soul space

WHERE GOD BREAKS IN

JEROME DALEY

INTEGRITY®
PUBLISHERS
Nashville

soulspace

Unless otherwise indicated, Scripture quotations in this volume are taken from the Holy Bible, New International Version (NIV). Copyright © 1973, 1978, 1984 by the International Bible Society. Used by permission of Zondervan Publishing House. All rights reserved. Other Scripture quotations are from the following sources:

The King James Version (KJV) of the Bible.

The Message (MSG), copyright © 1993, 1994, 1995, 1996, 2000, 2001, 2002. Used by permission of NavPress Publishing Group.

The New American Standard Bible (NASB), copyright © 1960, 1962, 1963, 1971, 1972, 1973, 1975, 1977, 1995 by the Lockman Foundation. Used by permission.

Some names and details in anecdotes and illustrations within this volume have been changed to protect the identities of those involved.

"Somewhere in Montana," used by permission of Scott Vaughn, Flying W Wranglers, Colorado Springs, Colorado.

"Dive" by Steven Curtis Chapman, copyright © Peach Tree Songs 2/Sparrow Songs (admin. EMI Music Publishing). All rights reserved. Used by permission.

"I Hope You Dance," by Mark Sanders and Tia Sillers. Copyright © 2000 Universal-MAC Music Publishing, Inc. on behalf of Itself and Soda Creek Songs. All rights reserved. Used by permission.

Published in association with Kathy Helmers, Alive Communications, Colorado Springs, Colorado

Cover Design: The Office of Bill Chiaravalle
Interior Design: Inside Out Design & Typesetting

Library of Congress Cataloging-in-Publication Data

Daley, Jerome.
    Soul space : where God breaks in / by Jerome Daley
        p. cm.
    ISBN 1-59145-035-7
    1. Spiritual life—Christianity. 2. Daley, Jerome. I. Title.

BV4501.3.D34   2002
248.4–dc21
                                                                                2002038833

Printed in the United States of America
03 04 05 06 07 RRD 9 8 7 6 5 4 3 2 1

To Kellie.

Truest friend and steadfast
companion.

My soulmate and one-flesh destiny.

Warrior and lover. Forever.

contents

chapter one

Life Has Got Me by the Tail, and It Won't Let Go

My heart is racing and my knees are weak as I walk to the edge. I know there is no turning back once my feet have left the ledge. And in the rush I hear a voice that's telling me to take the leap of faith, so here I go. . . .

—"Dive"
STEVEN CURTIS CHAPMAN

WE SAT ACROSS FROM ONE ANOTHER face to face in a generic diner in a small town in North Carolina. For the past year there had been a rising tide of realization within me that was now overflowing the retaining walls of my denial, and I realized—with a twinge of panic—that we were not living life, but that life was living us. That no matter how good it might appear on the surface, we were no longer in charge. Life had got us by the tail, and it wouldn't let go! As my eyes met Kellie's across the table, we connected in a silent moment of life-changing decision: *We've got to get out!*

For me, the decision came with the breaking reality that our marriage was deteriorating, our children were not getting the fathering they desperately needed, and my work in the church—among truly wonderful men and women—was not satisfying my sense of destiny. Most unnerving of all, my soul was so awash in busyness that I was no longer sure who the real me was. *In fact,* I wondered, *have I ever really known my true self . . . or is my life to date simply a careless collection of miscellaneous desires, vague abilities, and other people's expectations?* As Kellie and I faced one another that cool March evening, for the first time in my life I knew I could leave. I could leave my job and my world and go anywhere—anywhere with her, anywhere with God. The dark, green-brown eyes of my wife of nine years reflected back to me the truth that we needed a serious change from the cluttered and driven life we were living. Oh, it was a good life to be sure—a beautiful home, a loved and respected position as worship pastor, my black convertible . . . now *that* was something most pastors didn't drive!

We stared at each other. What would it all mean? Surely it wasn't practical to consider uprooting ourselves. *Practical*—I had come to hate that word! Nevertheless, we would have to pray a lot over this one. Even though we were afraid to verbalize it— afraid of what it might cost us—a hope sprang up deep within us, and we both knew without saying it: We were leaving. This was not just a geographical leaving but a soul-leaving—a retreat

> *This was a soul-leaving . . . a renunciation of the gerbil wheel!*

from the gerbil wheel, no . . . something more violent . . . a *renunciation* of the gerbil wheel! No matter how impractical it might be, no matter how many people wouldn't understand, no matter what it might cost us financially and relationally—we were pulling the plug on life as we knew it.

We knew this process couldn't be done quickly. But we weren't out for a quick fix. Instead we took three days to carefully consider what we were planning; during those days we settled in our hearts that we would take a year, a full twelve months, to go find our souls, our family, and our God!

What about you? Is your marriage suffering, as ours was? Are your children losing the parenting they so desperately need? Is your work filling every moment of your life with tremendous busyness that, nonetheless, leaves you dissatisfied and searching? If you're ready to get off your gerbil wheel, you'll find plenty of company in these pages. I hope to encourage you to root out the things that clutter and poison your soul. I want to help you realize that you do have choices and the power to make the choice for space within your life and your soul. And I hope to show you that the lasting rewards to be found in this space will become far more compelling than a life of clutter and distraction.

What is it exactly that I want to help you make space for? My goal is to help you identify what is *truly most important*. As Jesus said to one of His closest friends, "You are worried and bothered about so many things, but only a few things are necessary" (Luke 10:41–42 NASB).

Only a few things are necessary! The rest is clutter.

Does it sound like I'm suggesting radical changes? Yes, I suppose so. But don't knock radical. Simple adjustments require simple changes; life-changing corrections usually require bone-jarring, teeth-rattling transitions that are not pretty and not easy. Don't worry. I'm not suggesting that you have to take a year off to pursue your own freedom from distractions and busyness; but in some form you *will* have to draw on the courage to make radical changes of your own.

Everyday habits—our patterns of relating to our spouses, our routines of work and leisure, our responses to stress, our self-talk—these things are rooted so deeply inside us that most of us go through life unaware and unchanged at this root level—unless something radical happens. In fact, I discovered that even though I am a thoughtful and analytical kind of guy, I did not understand, and therefore could not fix, the underlying motivations and frustrations of my heart. I wanted to change, but I couldn't. Why was this? Was I alone in the club of the clueless? I have come to think not.

There is a reason why so many people, Christians and non-Christians alike, have lost contact with their souls. There is a soul anesthesia that pervades the atmosphere of our daily lives and affects us all. You don't have to look far to find the evidence. It's in the automatic greetings and responses we trade with one another daily:

"Hi, Joe," you say. "How've you been?"

It's a generic question, right? Usually it elicits a generic answer. And the automatic, generic response is, "Well, I've been _____."
You fill in the answer. There's only one, and you know what it is: "I've been *busy!*" How many times has the word come out of your mouth? How many times has it come out of mine? Busyness is the dulling reality that keeps us locked into soul-less living. But what are we willing to do about it? Ah, that is the question! Freedom from soul clutter is not so far away, once we set our hearts on having it. But jumping off that gerbil wheel takes thought—and effort.

IN THE GRIP OF BUSYNESS

The grip of busyness endures for three reasons: the values of the world system, our desperate yearning for control, and the addictive nature of the beast. Or, to put it more succinctly: greed, fear, and pride—the pillars of all destructive behavior and the things that most grieve the heart of God.

Busyness is the drug of choice for modern America. I know it was mine. It's a rare soul indeed who hasn't succumbed to the tantalizing allure of *production.* "Do more! Do it faster!" is the anthem of modern advertisers. Day-timers, cell phones, laptops, pagers, personal digital assistants—they're all helping us get ahead, get organized, and, well, produce!

Busyness has the ability to bring with it a distinct "high," a momentary sense of significance, an emotional rush that can feel exhilarating, even intoxicating. And though we hate it at times, we also crave it the way drug addicts hate and love the source of their addictions. We never really challenge or question the way this addictive busyness dominates our days. Instead, we elevate it as a proud trophy of our accomplishment. And we stay trapped inside that gerbil wheel as it keeps on spinning . . .

The "world system"—that structure that motivates and directs the ambitions of people—is built upon the pursuit of power and possession. To put it bluntly, it's a system based on greed. As Christians, we live within a broken world and yet are not to be ruled by its broken system (see John 17:15–16). But it's not so easy to escape this system, is it? It's in the corporate air we breathe; it's in the relational fabric we live in. Essentially, its seeds are lodged in our own hearts. Most of us have been lulled half asleep by this system of thinking, by a set of priorities and assumptions that are not rooted in the Kingdom of God yet are unwittingly adopted into the daily lives of Godward men and women.

Further, busyness grips us because of our grip on control . . . because our fears compel us to attempt that which we cannot actually accomplish: to control the parameters of our lives. We are plagued by the feeling of being "out of control," and it terrifies us! Thus we have an urgent drive to enforce and defend our will in the complex machinery of life. But it rarely works. We run faster but make little progress.

QUESTIONS THAT REQUIRE SPACE

Caught up in the daily demands of ministry, I thrived on the challenges and activities of the church. Ministry, like many other jobs, is never done; there is a constant and genuine cry for more and better. When you come to the end of the day, you have to stop . . . but you're not finished.

Between the push and pull of love and duty, ministry was all-consuming and left little time for me to ask myself such frivolous questions as, *Why am I here? I know I am serving God and serving people, but what am I ultimately made for?* These are questions that require space for considering—room in the mind, space in the soul. Soulspace. A protected reserve of unallocated thinking, feeling, and willing. Soulspace is room to think, time to reflect, freedom to evaluate.

To create this space I had to carve out a refuge to consciously *be* rather than *do*. As I sat with Kellie that Tuesday night over dinner, considering our future, I had little space left in my life. Instead I had clutter. Clutter is the opposite of space. Clutter is the chaotic jumble of life that forces us automatically forward into the next task, denying us the opportunity to rest, refocus, and re-engage upon our true calling. Fortunately for Kellie and me, our life-clutter had crossed the threshold of pain, and through that discomfort we felt a motivation we had never felt before.

Sometimes pain is our best friend.

JOINING THE RANKS OF THE NEEDY

The pastoral staff I worked with could not understand our decision to leave. These were all good men, godly men, leading a church whose goal was to change a city, but the staff members' general consensus was, *Why can't you just work it out?* One of them offered the visualization that when an athlete sprains his ankle, he doesn't sit out the season but gets back on the field to work it out.

My response was, "That's true, but if his leg is broken, then the rules change. He needs an emergency room, and if it's bad enough, he'll need physical therapy for months before he's back out on that field." I knew in my heart that we were headed for spiritual ER and heart-therapy.

My great desire is that you can go to school on me, gleaning from my experience the hard-earned lessons of my journey so that you can stay in the game.

We need to know what's broken in our lives and how bad it is before we can determine how to go about getting healed. The problem is that very few among us will admit to being broken. Even in the church—the assembly of the broken—it is often considered bad form to "bleed" on one another, to admit the depth of our brokenness. There are the acceptable sins—worry, anger, lack of discipline, even lust. But when you dig a little deeper and begin acknowledging your very poverty of soul, your elusive identity, and your unresolved woundedness, you frequently enter the domain of the spiritually illegitimate and socially orphaned—the marginalized people who we know need our help but that we're not anxious to be around, the "extra-grace-required" folks (as one leadership book delicately phrases it)—candidates for inner healing. As if we don't all need to be healed, inside and out.

Kellie and I didn't even know how to verbalize such thoughts as these; we only saw that we were dying inside and needed some intensive, focused soulcare. Within three months, we had rented out our house, thrown our stuff in a truck, loaded three kids and two cats in the van, and driven sixteen hundred miles to a city where we knew four people, barely. After three days on the road, we spent our first chaotic night in Colorado Springs, packed into the Hampton Inn with the kids and the cats, all of whom were whining and fighting, all our nerves raw.

The next day we began scouting houses for rent. We found nothing, and finally, in frustration, I just pulled over to the side of the road. Kellie and I wordlessly asked ourselves, *Why are we here? What have we done? Are we crazy?* Yes, it was a dramatic and awful moment! As I recall, some of the kids were crying, and I think both Kellie and I were crying too. It wasn't so much the house situation as just the accumulation of stress triggered by the moment.

Imagining that distraught scene on the Colorado roadside, perhaps you can understand now why I said earlier that life-changing corrections often require bone-jarring, teeth-rattling transitions that are not pretty and are not easy. At that moment in that place, we were closer to despair than I ever want to be again. We were on the edge of a life-changing correction, but it felt like we were teetering on the edge of a precipice. Would we step off that precipice in faith, knowing that whatever happened to us out there in Colorado, God would see us through? Or would we give up and return to the addictive busyness that was so reassuringly familiar? Would we climb back onto the gerbil wheel? Or would we continue our quest?

THE QUEST TO FILL THE GOD-SHAPED HOLE

A quest is a search for something, usually something of great value, that takes us on a journey over time and across formidable obstacles to finally lay hold of the prize—that compelling object of our passion. In this concept of quest I see glimmers of excitement, shadows of danger, and the sure promise of adventure. (I also see a car parked beside the road with some very anxious people inside questioning their own sanity—but we'll get back to them later.)

What is your quest? What is your passion? Is it a search motivated by greed, fear, and pride? Or is it a quest that pulls you toward God?

There is an explorer hidden inside each of us, hard-wired into our fundamental design as an ability and a yearning to discover. This curiosity, this desire to "search out," is most obvious in us during childhood. As we grow up, this yearning tends to get either cultivated or squelched, depending upon our soul structures and those who influence us. But it doesn't die. If we're wise, if we're encouraged, this tendency evolves into a desire to find God and to fill our lives, our souls, with Him. It becomes a quest that leaves us restless and driven to fill the God-shaped hole in our lives. As Saint Augustine wrote, "Thou hast formed us for Thyself, and our hearts are restless till they find rest in Thee."

There is an explorer hidden inside each of us, an ability and yearning to discover.

It's something like the restless stirring and determination illustrated in Sheila Burnford's heartwarming story *The Incredible Journey*, in which a Labrador retriever, a bull terrier, and a Siamese cat cross three hundred miles of Canadian wilderness, as though following an invisible tracker beam, to find their home and family. The fact is, sometimes animals are smarter than we humans. Sometimes a pet can be truer to its heart-home than people are!

Still, we struggle on in pursuit of our quest. I suspect that a restless stirring in you caused you to pick up this book. Are you willing to take the risk of acknowledging your soul-lessness and to pursue your heart again? If you seek it, you can find it (see Matthew 7:7)!

"'It is the glory of God to conceal a matter; to search out a matter is the glory of kings" (Proverbs 25:2). God's favorite game, our pastor, Ted Haggard, loves to say, is hide-and-seek. He shows Himself to all men and women: to some more, to some less—but always enough to invite them into the search.

If they desire it. . . . if they want to engage.

But the question must be asked: Why? Why does God want us to search for Him? If God really wants to be with us so badly, why would He hide Himself? Why would it feel so hard at times to find Him?

Look at it this way: What are great kings and leaders known for? Their biggest conquests? Their greatest accomplishments? Or their smallest ones? Kings have always known that the greatest glory lies in the pursuit of the greatest riches across the greatest obstacles. That which takes little effort to grasp, we value lightly. But if we are motivated to go through the hassle of putting on the armor and saddling up the horse, and then to risk facing the dragons, we stand a good chance of finding the treasure. If we're not so motivated, we assuredly won't find it. Truly, God loves it when we yearn for Him and when we overcome obstacles to seek Him out. "Come near to God," James says, "and he will come near to you" (James 4:8). God is just waiting to break into our worlds.

On that Tuesday night in a nondescript grill, we pulled on our armor and saddled up to begin our quest in earnest. And there on the highway in Colorado, we met our first dragon.

Ours was not a running away from problems, but rather an intentional running toward the life we knew we were destined for. While our goal is the same—a desire to replace the clutter in our souls with the abundant presence of God—your quest will look different from ours. Everyone's story is unique. God wants to take each of us by the hand, wherever we are, and lead us into the freedom and purpose for which we are made. As you peer through this window into our story, let the Holy Spirit call to your heart and draw your soul into the kind of space He has custom-crafted for you!

THAT DIFFICULT FIRST STEP

We have talked about beginning a quest and the good things that await us at the end of this journey. But the truth is that it's sometimes hard to leave . . . hard to say good-bye to the familiar and the known. *It may be messy, but at least it's my mess!*

Unfortunately—or fortunately—to journey forward requires an absolute commitment, a fierce determination to break free of the tyranny of this world's system. You cannot reform this system, so don't even attempt superficial fixes. This system is devilish in the truest sense and cannot be trusted. This "leaving" may be internal and hidden, but it is very, very real! You cannot *go* somewhere without *leaving* somewhere; it's just a fact.

What's more, it's all or nothing. You cannot recreationally "dabble" in this new world of freedom, for one important reason: The old system is pervasive in its values and thinking, and you cannot shake its influence without adopting a radically new mentality. If you scrutinize this new thinking, this new set of values, while under allegiance to the old system, it will appear as foolishness. Totally impractical.

Jesus called this new system the "Kingdom of God," and it was the focal point of His message on earth. He brought to earth an entirely new way of living and loving and relating, but ultimately it was a new administration. A new King! And we cannot take a new king without leaving behind the old one. There is an intrinsic competition and hostility between these two kingdoms. Describing this conflict, Jesus said, "No one can serve two masters. Either he will hate the one and love the other, or he will be devoted to the one and despise the other" (Matthew 6:24).

Many well-intentioned Christians look to the world to tell them how to spend their time, money, and affections.

Yet this "dual citizenship" is the practical outworking of many well-intentioned Christians who welcome the rule of Christ in their lives but unwittingly look to the world to tell them how to spend their time, spend their money, and spend their affections. As a result, many Christians—like their neighbors—live harried and fragmented lives, driven in their pursuit of non-eternal goals and plagued by broken, shallow relationships.

Anybody want to leave *that* behind?

Just to be clear, the Kingdom life that Jesus holds out to us is not a pain-free life. The Kingdom God offers is a place of great joy and meaning in the midst of the sufferings of this world. One day we will awaken in the fullness of His Kingdom—heaven—and the pain will be gone. In the meantime, He beckons us to leave behind the anesthesia of this world's clutter and open our souls to the life of the Spirit.

On that day of decision, Kellie and I walked to the edge and decided that the pain and risk of leaping was less than the pain and risk of going back. It was time to dive!

SOULSPACE PRESCRIPTION

Over today's lunch hour or during the kids' nap time, instead of trying to check one more thing off the to-do list, get alone and ask yourself two questions:

1. What's broken in my life?

2. How committed am I to fixing it?

chapter two

Stripped to the Bone,
Regrounded in God

In contemporary society our Adversary majors in three things: noise, hurry, and crowds. If he can keep us engaged in "muchness" and "manyness," he will rest satisfied.

—RICHARD FOSTER

THE INCONVENIENT RUMBLINGS of my soul had begun several years prior. They would usually emerge as stomach-knotting frustrations and eventual eruptions of anger . . . about anything! The lawn mower breaking. A deadline missed. An e-mail lost. *Why?* I wondered. *There seems to be this ugly vat of anger that lies just below the carefully cultivated surface of my soul, and it keeps popping up in all these different areas and situations. Why?* Basically, one part of my life would cease to function, and the whole house of cards would wobble and threaten to come down. *I just can't hold it all together!* was my inner cry. The conviction settled upon my soul that, no matter how hard I worked or how organized I became, no matter how many time-management seminars I attended, I absolutely could not do and be everything I wanted to.

Well, this was unacceptable! Didn't God want me to succeed? What was all that scripture about the abundant life of the Spirit?

Time-management tools, for all their insight, can actually exacerbate the problem of soul clutter by reinforcing the false impression that you *can* do it all . . . if you will just list and prioritize all your tasks on those specially formatted and beautifully illustrated calendar pages! What I've learned in my journey is that, as powerful as prioritizing is, the cluttered or stress-diseased soul must be stripped to the bone and regrounded upon a solid foundation of God and self before there is any capacity to set healthy goals and priorities again.

Perhaps you are experiencing some of that stripping in your life these days.

TAKING A SABBATICAL

In the fall of 1998, the pastoral staff in the church where I worked was experimenting with the, for us, novel concept of sabbaticals. Though it was foreign to our corporate culture, the admonition of a "church-management expert" had prompted us to begin scheduling a one-month sabbatical for each of our pastors. I was desperate for such a retreat and hungrily scanned the calendar for my chance. After waiting my turn, May of 1999 became my door of opportunity, and my heart rose with expectation. And even though I was still laden with several responsibilities throughout that month, I plunged vigorously into the sabbatical, enjoying solitude, prayer, reflection, and evaluation. It was a foretaste of freedom, and it tasted good! Several of my soul infections became evident during that time, and I emerged from that month

It was a foretaste of freedom . . .

with the determination to make changes. *Finally!* I thought, *I have returned to the core of who I am and what I am about.*

With zeal, I set a new schedule of monthly prayer days. I resigned as vice president of our church network's training school. I dropped my favorite hobby of designing in-house publications. I created a transition plan to extricate myself from administrative responsibilities in the office. However, six months later I had to admit that I had only scratched the surface, and although the pressures had eased in their intensity, the root ills—whatever they might be—were still alive and well in my soul.

Dear God, I thought, *where do I go from here?*

But such is the deceptive "beauty" of busyness: It "rescues" us from the turmoil of uncomfortable wrestling and numbs our souls through the dominating demands of the next activity.

Perhaps you are in need of some kind of sabbatical yourself. It's not just pastors and professors who have permission to do this, you know. Anyone can do it. And everyone should at one time or another. Maybe your sabbatical will be taking a weekend—two complete days—and finding someplace where you can be completely alone. Perhaps a mountain cabin or a hotel or a retreat center where you can rent a room. Maybe, with a little advance planning, you can take a week. (You might find that a week with God beats a week at Disney World!) Life-defining moments begin in such ways.

For me, that first sabbatical set the stage for an inner revolt. Not exactly what I was looking for, but definitely what I needed. The anger wasn't going away; I was, in fact, starting to become more attuned to it. Somehow, in my deepest heart, I knew I needed to find something, my "one thing."

A "ONE THING" LIFE

On the day that Martha complained about her sister, Mary, sitting around at Jesus' feet instead of helping her prepare the meal for their guests, Jesus reached out with a word of comfort: "You are worried and bothered about so many things," He said tenderly, "but only a few things are necessary . . ." (Luke 10:41–42 NASB).

Only a few things? Really?

And then He continued, ". . . . really only one."

What is that one thing, that most necessary thing in life, the one thing that should lie at the core of our existence? Not surprisingly, the *thing* is actually a Person (and *people* will always, always, always be more important than *things*; we would do well to learn that truth sooner rather than later). The "one thing" Jesus was commending Mary for was simply sitting at His feet. Mary had made fellowship with her Lord the one necessary thing; food could take care of itself, obligations could wait, and other "pressing" concerns could be put on hold as long as she could just be with Him. For Mary, the "one thing" wasn't preparing a meal; it was preparing a soul—making room in her life for the life of God! Martha got lost in life's clutter while Mary made space for what was truly important.

You may have heard this story from Luke 10 a hundred times, but until you are sitting on the floor beside Mary, keep reading!

There are several biblical windows into this "one thing" idea, this compelling center of life around which our souls orbit. David said, "*One thing* I ask of the LORD, this is what I seek: that I may dwell in the house of the LORD all the days of my life, to gaze upon the beauty of the LORD and to seek him" (Psalm 27:4, emphasis added). Relationship with the Most High—could it be possible? Intimacy with the Almighty? If this is truly available, shouldn't it be our highest pursuit, the prize of life?

Giving Up in Order to Gain

Paul thought so. He wrote, "*One thing* I do: Forgetting what is behind and straining toward what is ahead, I press on toward the goal to win the prize for which God has called me heavenward in Christ Jesus" (Philippians 3:13–14, emphasis added). But what was the goal? What was the prize? He had already defined it a couple of verses earlier: "I want to know Christ" (v. 10). This desire was the driving force behind the early church's greatest apostle. Not planting churches. Not even evangelizing the world. Paul's deepest hunger was to sit at Jesus' feet, beside Mary as it were, and drink in the very presence and person of God Himself. This is the power for changing the world.

My friend Larry recently told me that this soulspace idea sounds good, but there's a cost—you have to give up some things in order to gain the space. How right he is! Listen to Paul's comment: "All the things I once thought were so important are gone from my life. Compared to the high privilege of knowing Christ Jesus as my Master, firsthand, everything I once thought I had going for me is insignificant—dog dung. I've dumped it all in the trash so that I could embrace Christ and be embraced by him" (Philippians 3:7–8 MSG). The Daley version of this insight is, "All the stuff I used to spend my greatest time and energy pursuing—that stuff is clutter! But Jesus—now *He* is worth *everything*, so I'll do *anything* to make space in my soul for Him!"

Paul found his "one thing." How's it going for you?

The Wake-up Call

God has broken into my world in several unforgettable moments.
The story I'll relate to you now is about one of those moments; it was
the awakening of my "one thing." I was
thirteen. Eighth grade. I had grown up
wanting to know and love God to the
best of my ability . . . but it felt harder
now. Some of my friends were making
choices that I knew would take them
away from God, not toward Him.
Drinking, smoking, listening to ques-
tionable music—not exactly hard-core
evil, but the fork in the path was obvious. I stopped, unsure. What
would that path hold? How could I continue the path I was on
without knowing where other paths would lead?

There's a cost!
You have to give up
some things in order to
gain the space

Then I had a sleepover with one of my junior high buddies, and
together with a third friend, we lived it up, thirteen-year-old style. I
tried my first swallow of whiskey—and was that ever an unpleasant
surprise! But still very cool, of course. By the middle of the night, my
soul—and my head—were reeling in a cloud of cigarette smoke and
vertigo from hours of late-night TV. Were we having fun yet?

Then something deep inside me cried out, *This is not what I was
made for! Dad, please come take me home!* The thought of actually
calling home crossed my mind. *No, can't do that; definitely uncool.* So
I gutted it out until the next morning when Dad did come to pick me
up in our old Ford sedan, roughly the size of a Third World country.
By that time, the inner crisis had passed in its intensity, and I was
feeling a bit numb as we drove through the neighborhood.

"How was your time with the guys?" I'm sure Dad asked.

"Fine," I'm sure I replied.

Then he said something I'll never forget. "You know, a strange thing happened to me last night," Dad said casually. "I woke up in the middle of the night, and it was almost like I could hear you calling me."

Well, that did it! Between the gushing sobs, I managed to get out my story. Dad listened compassionately. I don't remember anything else he actually said, but I will always remember that night. I think of it as the night God called my name. It may have been my dad that God woke up, but it was me He was calling. And I heard Him loud and clear. The peace and contentment that flooded my soul that day were like nothing I had ever known. *He cares about me! A very big God really likes me a lot to go to all the trouble of waking up my dad because I was hurting!* I knew on that late-spring day of 1979 that I had my "one thing" to live for. And that has never changed. But still, the clutter in life came hard and fast back then—as it does today.

DISCIPLINE: FRIEND OR FOE?

During my sabbatical of May 1999, I spent a week alone at the beach, trying to sort through my soul clutter. It was kind of like cleaning out the garage: *Keep this, throw away that. What is that? Hey! I haven't seen that in two years!*

One of the long-term benefits of that sabbatical—an issue that emerged from the shadows one day as I watched a crane glide awkwardly over the coastal bay—was my shift in thinking about discipline. Not discipline in the sense of punishment but of training. Discipline had always been held up for me as the key to the Christian life; in fact, I see that thinking in many parts of the body of Christ. Because it is indeed a powerful tool, it is often regarded as something of a "holy grail" in the journey toward spirituality.

Because discipline has never been my strong suit, the rub was a consistent, low-grade frustration over whatever part of my life wasn't working at a given moment. I thought, *If I could just get up earlier . . . If I could just pray longer . . . If I could just have been better prepared for that church event . . . Why can't I be this incredibly disciplined person? Why can't I be super-pastor? Isn't that the goal? Wouldn't that make God happy? I'm sure it would make people happy. I know it would make me happy . . . wouldn't it?*

Today I continue to find discipline to be a topic of great interest among those who are set upon following God. Of course, for "recreational Christians"—those who treat God as a nice hobby—this subject is quickly and decisively avoided. But those who deeply hunger for God have a great desire to train themselves in the pursuit of God. The knight who goes out to slay the dragon and rescue the princess surely comes to appreciate the hours of riding lessons, sword training, and tactical instruction he received.

Discipline had always been held up for me as the key to the Christian life.

My first question was this: Is discipline, in the sense of strict behavioral (not moral) boundaries, a true biblical virtue? In other words, does the Bible call us to rigid structures of spiritual routine as a foundation for Kingdom living? A word search uncovered that, although the word is used extensively in Scripture, it almost always refers to discipline in the alternate sense of correction or punishment. Jesus Himself seems to have avoided the topic almost entirely, focusing instead on heart issues. To me, this speaks volumes! Paul referred to discipline in the sense of training oneself in godliness (see 1 Timothy 4:7–8) and used the concept of discipline, if not the word, in 1 Corinthians 9:24–27, as he described the rigors of training oneself for a race. So discipline does have a small but valid biblical role in our spiritual development.

But . . . can discipline ignite the quest for more of God in our lives? Does discipline lead us to intimacy? That is the next question.

When Duty Substitutes for Desire

Despite God's cry for intimacy, the epitome of our Christian experience is often the guilt-ridden cycle of attempting to read the Bible and pray more often . . . and then failing miserably. Why is that? What is so wrong with us that keeps men and women of God, often ten and twenty years into their Christian walk, still struggling under the burden of ought and obligation? Many, it seems, would answer, "No, those disciplines don't work for me." Why is that?

I answer it this way. First, because the very Scriptures and prayer that are indeed our lifelines to God are still the *conduit* to life, not life itself. So when duty substitutes for desire, we are left with a hollow shell of performance-motivated slavery.

Just compare the frowning Pharisee with the wild-eyed, ecstatic lover of the Song of Solomon. Case closed!

Second, because it's easier to teach structures than relationship, our spiritual leaders frequently focus their attention on the former. So we focus *our* attention there as well.

Third, discipline fails because our own hearts betray us and opt for the emotional crutch of pursuing spiritual activity as a substitute for the emotionally vulnerable and time-consuming option of pursuing a Person.

Finally, we choose "devotions" over devotion because we have seen so little of how beautiful and wonderful our heavenly Lover truly is.

THE SOURCE OF PASSION

Passion doesn't exist in a vacuum. Instead, passion begins with a vision. It happens when the guy sees the girl and his heart starts to race and his palms sweat and his mind begins conjuring up excuses to meet her and hang around her! A blind date never sets the heart in motion like getting a glimpse of the real beauty beforehand. But when it comes to passion about our relationship with the Savior, by the time the image of Christ is filtered through the "line noise" of one hundred channels of satellite TV, we are left with a pretty low resolution picture that's not too compelling.

I got a vivid refresher course on this dynamic some months ago when we were back in our hometown to sell the house we had rented out the previous year. Leaving our TV-less home in Colorado, we were now spending two weeks with a large TV and cable. Planning to watch only a bit of TV during those two weeks, we were nevertheless sucked into dulling nightly mind-melds of inane programming. One night in particular, I drove myself nearly homicidal while flipping channels repeatedly for two hours—doggedly determined to find something worth watching but destined for failure.

Strangely, our morning times with God slacked off during those two weeks as our TV viewing increased. Hmmm . . .

Proverbs 29:18 is a well-known verse that says, "Where there is no vision, the people are unrestrained" (NASB). I think it's fair to the text to reverse the statement into a positive: Where there is vision, people are restrained. Discipline is restraint, but the potential for discipline cannot be activated without a compelling vision. Just think of your own experience with discipline—a diet begun, the gym membership purchased, a home-improvement project undertaken. We laugh at ourselves (and sometimes cry) over our inability to make those New Year's resolutions stick. But it's all about the vision, not the discipline. A strong-enough vision will transform the discipline into joy, but it rarely works in reverse!

The Danger of Discipline

Jack Deere, a former seminary professor and well-known author and speaker, relates how he came to a point of evaluation in his life where he had to acknowledge that all his years of Bible study and seminary teaching had not drawn him into intimacy with his heavenly Father. In fact, it hit him that some of the other professors who were most astute and studious in their knowledge of God were actually as "mean as snakes"![1] Nevertheless, the teaching is pervasive in the body of Christ that discipline of various types—prayer, Bible study, fasting, memorization—is the key to an intimate relationship with God. I have come to believe this is not the case.

In fact, I believe discipline can be a dangerous thing and requires careful watch in our hearts. Too great a focus upon discipline will, first of all, orient our activities around tasks instead of people. And the example of Christ, refreshing in this age of production, is that people are the focal point; tasks are secondary and only have meaning as they directly impact relationship. In addition, when we fail in our disciplines, we can easily believe that we have failed in our relationship with God. This may or may not be true. In other words, it is an open invitation to one of the most widespread hindrances in the Christian life: condemnation. On the other hand, if we are successful in our disciplines, we may easily come to measure our spiritual vitality by them, leading to pride and legalism.

It is not inconsequential that Jesus' primary adversaries were the religious legalists. Similarly, the Pharisee in us readily arises to the tune of discipline: *Do more for God, and do it better.* It's a dangerous stunt, trying to charm that beast. Discipline is the number one component of legalism, and legalism is the number one counterfeit to the life of the Spirit for which we long.

> *The example of Christ is that people are the focal point; tasks are secondary.*

So is discipline our foe? Not really. My relationship with God is stronger now than ever before in my life, and I can tell you I'm probably more disciplined now than before. I am getting up earlier than I ever have. I am spending more time in prayer than ever before. I follow a budget. I spend intentional time with my children. I structure my life according to God-breathed priorities.

So who—or what—*is* our foe? Condemnation is our foe—the voice of the enemy telling us that we are failures and might as well give up. Legalism is definitely our foe—the voice of the enemy whispering that because we do this or that for God we have merited His favor (and by the way, why can't everybody else get his or her act together?).

How Discipline Becomes Our Friend and Ally

Well then, for crying out loud, what are we to think of discipline? Discipline is a valuable tool, but like most tools, we need to understand its function and its limitations. Discipline is powerful in training and equipping our minds with God's truth, as Paul's letters tell us. Discipline can focus our wills. Ultimately, the power of discipline is its ability as a soul-tool to call us away from distraction and back to the vision—to encourage our pursuit by causing us to look more deeply, more carefully, and more longingly at the Love of our lives! This vision is the only force strong enough to sustain discipline day in, day out, year in, year out. And it is as we see Him and know Him that discipline becomes our friend, our ally in the quest!

A more biblical word than *discipline*, I have come to believe, is *self-control*. This character quality is included in the prominent list of "fruit of the Spirit" in Galatians 5 and has numerous other references. So what is the difference between discipline and self-control? Well, it can be subtle, but Paul's letter to the Galatians gave me a clue: Self-control is a fruit of the Spirit, whereas discipline can be a fruit of human effort. I began to notice that in the term *self-control*, the word *self* was the object, not the subject. That meant that it was not *me* who was doing the controlling, but my *self* that was actually being controlled—by the Holy Spirit!

This doesn't mean that I have no part in the process, because of course I do. But it does mean that I am neither the initiator nor the empowerer of self-control; rather, I embrace and support the work of God within me, knowing that self-discipline is a tool that can assist me toward the character quality of self-control, which produces freedom in my life.

Before we go on to the next chapter, I'd like to challenge you to evaluate your own relationship within the dynamics of discipline and self-control. More importantly, assess whether you understand your motivations behind both your successes and your failures in this realm. It is crucial to be very clear on our heart condition here.

ESCAPING THE TRAP

In our heart of hearts, we know that we are not free. But freedom is what Jesus came to give us; it was—and is—His mission. He defined His own ministry through the words of Isaiah the prophet:

> The Spirit of the LORD is on me, because he has anointed me to preach good news to the poor. He has sent me to proclaim freedom for the prisoners and recovery of sight for the blind, to release the oppressed, to proclaim the year of the Lord's favor. (Luke 4:18–19)

We must embrace this gift of God—that we can choose what will be important to us.

We are the poor, the imprisoned, the blind, and the oppressed—until He sets us free. He came to make us rich, to emancipate us, to envision us, and to liberate us! Yet we often feel trapped in a life we cannot shape. We feel like life shapes us, as if we have no control over its rule. And while there are many things in life we can't control, we do have the power of choice . . . more than we think!

Before we go any further in our journey toward soulspace, we must realize and embrace this gift of God—that we *can* choose what will be important to us. We *can* choose how we will spend our spiritual resources of time and money. We *can* choose to sit at the feet of Jesus and make intimacy with Him the greatest priority of our lives! So, in the great words of the knight guarding the chalice from Indiana Jones, I urge you to "choose wisely"!

If we neglect the God-given power of choice, we will drift down the river of life in a world crafted by others, banging into rocks, injuring ourselves and others without knowing why. But if we are to succeed on this journey, we must say "No!" to that life and forge a new course, cutting upstream through the buried debris.

In the next chapter we'll study head-on that dreaded enemy of debris: life clutter!

SOULSPACE PRESCRIPTION

Before you go to sleep tonight, grab some paper and write an answer to these three questions:

1. What really important thing am I passionate about?

2. What choices am I making to create space for that passion?

3. Am I making other choices based upon external forces and expectations that are not authentic to my own heart?

chapter three

The Clutter
Strikes Back

The old question, "What is the chief end of man?" is now
answered, "To dash around the world and add to the din thereof."
Speed and noise are evidences of weakness, not strength. The
desire to be dramatically active is proof of our religious infanti-
lism; it is a type of exhibitionism common to the kindergarten.

—A. W. TOZER

FOLLOWING MY MINI-SABBATICAL, I struggled to chart a
new course for myself. What I found, after the initial rush of
adrenaline, was that clutter was deeply embedded in my soul and
was actually a part of me. I would drop this activity or that responsibility, but I continued to remain unfocused and unsatisfied,
though I would only realize this in rare, unguarded moments. Brent
Curtis and John Eldredge describe it this way in their soul-searching
book, *The Sacred Romance:*

The voice often comes in the middle of the night or the early hours
of morning, when our hearts are most unedited and vulnerable. At
first, we mistake the source of this voice and assume it is just our
imagination. We fluff up our pillow, roll over, and go back to sleep.
Days, weeks, even months go by and the voice speaks to us again:
Aren't you thirsty? Listen to your heart. There is something missing.[1]

Dr. Richard Swenson's diagnosis is that "modern-day living opposes focusing. Surrounded by frenzy and interruptions, we have no time for anything but vertigo."[2] And Tommy Tenney declares, "Most of us keep our lives so jammed with junk food for the soul and amusements for the flesh that we don't know what it is to be really hungry [for God]."[3]

These writers are describing what I call clutter, soul clutter. It's the overwhelming "stuff" of life that captures our energies while we watch more important, but less urgent, things slide by untended. This phenomenon was the subject of a brilliant book by Charles Hummel some thirty years ago entitled *The Tyranny of the Urgent.* What a telling title! Deadlines, crises, conflicts, mistakes, breakages, interruptions—they all cry out for our attention throughout the day: *Me! Now! Give me your attention!* And so we do.

The important things in life, meanwhile, are rarely urgent—a date night with your spouse, your child's insecurity at school, dealing with a personal sin that is sabotaging your soul. Stress-relievers like exercise and recreation are usually the first to be jettisoned when the heat cranks up. We rationalize magnificently that this is just a "busy season" of life and soon things will return to normal. Come on, be honest. You know you do it! Most of us do. Our capacity for self-deception is off the charts.

And so the seasons go by, our children grow up, and we get older. The clutter changes shape and wears new clothes, but it never leaves home.

My personal clutter was exacerbated by my unbounded vision. I wanted to do everything . . . and do it well, of course. I wanted to write and record worship music, so I began building a recording studio only to have it sit idle for almost two years. I wanted to assist other worship leaders, so I helped organize a citywide worship group and citywide worship events. I organized and taught a school of worship for our network of churches. I wanted to add on to our house, so I drew elaborate plans; I wanted to landscape my backyard, so I studied landscape design and drafted detailed schemes. I wanted to refine our personnel plans at the church, so I poured many hours into painstaking human-resource charts showing who to hire and how to reorganize the staff. And of course as wor-

The important things in life are rarely urgent.

ship pastor, I had to prepare for at least three weekly services, organize and practice with the bands, attend frequent pastors meetings, lead small groups, and counsel and pastor my leadership team. In between those duties, I prepared budgets for the church, fertilized my lawn, went to conferences, changed diapers, preached periodically, and tried to keep the checkbook balanced.

If it sounds like the life I have described was unworkable, that's because it was. I don't have to tell you that I constantly felt like I was behind (which was always true) and out of control (usually true). It was like trying to keep a dozen tennis balls underwater in a pool; as soon as I would secure several here, a couple would pop to the surface there. You know the story because it's your story, too—just change the details and fill in the blanks. It's another verse in the hit song, "You Can Have It All," sung by most of the people we live beside, carpool our girls to ballet with, and go to church with.

Have you figured out yet that it's a lie?

If you can relate to this scenario, then pause for a minute . . . and let the question wash over you: *Do I want to live my life this way?*

We do have a choice, you and I. We can allow our culture and ego to tear at the edges of our souls until we are living on a mere scrap of our true selves. Or we can play by another set of rules. The rules of the Kingdom of God.

DIAGNOSING OUR CONDITION

Why do we so consistently revert to the lie? My answer is because our thinking and our motivations are programmed by—surprise!— the world system. There is a passage in 1 John 2 that lays bare the roots of this system, and it is important that we understand the root issues within ourselves that rob our quality of life:

> Do not love the world [system] or anything in the world [that operates by its rules]. If anyone loves the world, the love of the Father is not in him [because these kingdoms are diametrically opposed]. For everything in the world—the cravings of sinful man [fear-based], the lust of his eyes [greed-based] and the boasting of what he has and does [pride-based]—comes not from the Father but from the world. The world and its desires pass away, but the man who does the will of God lives forever. (vv. 15–17)

The world system—the rules by which people and organizations operate (without God)—is rooted in these three things: fear, greed, and pride. The motivation for accumulating pleasures and possessions is *pulled by greed, pushed by fear* (the anxiety of losing what we have or what we think we should have), and *powered by pride.* Applying that understanding to my own life, I see that my fragmentation and distraction were motivated by, well, a mixture of these factors. Certainly there were some good motivations for many of the activities I was engaged in. But intertwining my desires to honor God and help people were strains of fear (that I wasn't a good

World System Tree

FEAR PRIDE

GREED

enough pastor . . . or songwriter . . . or whatever), greed (for more influence and recognition), and pride (in the kingdom I was building for myself).

Such motivations are putrid to God. They stink! And of course they rob us of our intimacy with the Father that we so crave. They rob our families, and they rob our own souls. So, somehow, we have to learn how to x-ray our souls and put them up on the lightboard to diagnose our true condition.

The Outgrowths of Fear, Greed, and Pride

If fear, greed, and pride are the roots of the world system, they sprout up into three main "branches" of this tree: insecurity, materialism, and control.

Insecurity is an obvious outgrowth of fear, and the truth is that we all have insecurity within us. But whatever fruit is produced out of this heart-motivation of insecurity is going to be destructive—life-taking and not life-giving. I often felt insecure as a worship leader; the fear of failing to create a tangible encounter between God and the congregation was a very real, albeit irrational, motivation. It was irrational because we cannot manipulate God (and should not manipulate people). Leaders cannot create an encounter; they can only create an environment for an encounter. The manifestation of my insecurity was a reluctance to take risks in worship and an unhealthy dependency upon forms and programming. For example, it was often easier to stay within the safe confines of a preplanned song list than venture out into a spontaneous song selection where I might forget the words, where the musical transitions weren't pretty; and where I might not know where to go from there. The possibility of appearing awkward or foolish felt very tangible. Sometimes it still does. You can ponder and evaluate your own expressions of insecurity . . . if you dare!

Materialism is not just about the pursuit of money and toys. Materialism is also expressed in a preoccupation with quantity over quality and the tangible over the intangible. How does that work?

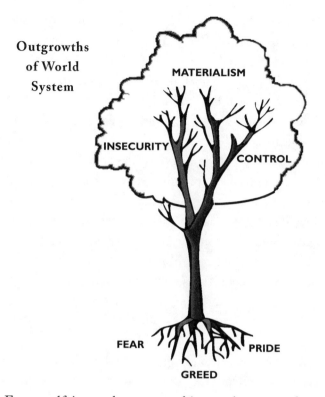

Outgrowths of World System

MATERIALISM

INSECURITY

CONTROL

FEAR

PRIDE

GREED

For myself, it was demonstrated in part by my need to accumulate more jobs in ministry—to validate myself as useful and necessary in the church. Doing more things at the expense of doing them well is an expression of materialism. This motivation also pushes us to produce tangible (material) things at the expense of the intangible; for me this formed the urgency to emphasize public programs and structures over prayer and personal intimacy with God.

Control is one of the most common expressions of pride (though it also draws greatly from our fears). Pride causes us, first, to assume that we have the definitive truth on all issues, and second, to then feel it necessary to squelch any competing views. Control moves us to feel that God can't quite keep our things and people in line, and He needs our help to do it. This quality can operate solely in our personal lives, where we attempt to engineer all the elements of our own lives toward our enlightened goals, or it can extend into trying to manage other people so as to further our personal objectives.

Granted, there can appear to be a fine line between leadership and control, but true leadership empowers other people toward common goals rather than usurping the gifts of others through micromanagement. My personal experience with control was channeled primarily into my futile attempts to manage my megavision. The only biblically approved control is self-control, by which we resist evil rather than manipulate our environments.

Getting Personal: The Symptoms of Soul Clutter

While it may be easy to understand this roots-and-branches analysis of the way the world system operates, it is sometimes less obvious how its fruit grows in our own lives; we frequently find it difficult to assess our own heart-motivations. So we have to look for more obvious symptoms. In my experience and observation, three primary indicators appear when we are living according to the world's system of rules; they are the "fruits" of soul clutter: drivenness, distraction, and superficiality.

Drivenness is characterized by frantic activity that is rooted most often in fear and developed through our insecurity: the fear of failure, the fear of rejection, the fear of not meeting someone else's (or your own) expectations. Drivenness may masquerade as industriousness, as a Type-A personality, or as godly commitment, but it will always be exposed by a lurking frustration. Drivenness is not a quality of the Kingdom of God. Passion is, perseverance is, determination is . . . but drivenness is not! If you regularly feel pressured, stressed, and always behind, then you probably struggle with drivenness.

Distraction is having too many targets, and most of them are moving. Too many goals, too much vision. Distraction is the opposite of focus, and it renders many of us impotent to accomplish the things to which we are truly called. Some people are better at multitasking

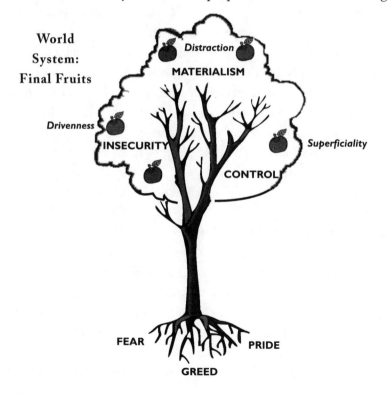

than others, but whatever our capacity, we have to narrow our attention to what is truly important in our lives and not allow the "urgent" to blind us to the "important." Of course, we all face crises and interruptions, but men and women of soulspace are known by how quickly they can refocus. Essential to defeating distraction is the ability to say no. The nicer you are, the harder this is! But at the foundation it is a people-pleasing motivation and a lack of clear identity that keeps us from saying no when we need to. If you are regularly taking on new responsibilities while the ones you already have are not healthy, then you probably qualify as distracted.

Superficiality develops when we become consumed with tasks instead of focused on people. Strong relationships are the greatest antidote to clutter. One of the sad realizations I had upon leaving my life of clutter in North Carolina was how very few vital friendships I had to show for thirteen years in that community. Upon discovering and grieving this reality, I made a commitment to never again live that way—to never lack for deep, meaningful friendships. But to do that, I had to rid myself of clutter and recapture the space necessary for these essential relationships.

My relationship with Kellie and our children was also hindered by the lack of space in my life. I was giving my family the emotional leftovers from my to-do lists. I would come home from work, frequently late, with my mind tied up in knots over the latest project and my soul drained from juggling the urgent. So, except for rare moments, I was unable to invest myself in the four people I most loved in this world. Isn't that one of the greatest tragedies of this world? Yet it probably is played out in the vast majority of homes in every neighborhood—maybe yours!

How about you? If your family is frequently going without

intentional, high-quality deposits of spouse-nurturing and kid-parenting, or if you have lots of "friends" but very little sharing and shaping of one another's lives, then you are probably living a superficial life just as I was.

FROM MYRIAD DISTRACTIONS TO A "ONE-THING" LIFE

If these destructive dynamics are *not* the forces you want working inside you, then you must bring the life and truth of God to bear upon their expressions within your soul. As you "speak" to your will to cool it, the Spirit of God within your spirit will leap to your aid to release you from drivenness, take hold of the peace of God, and guide you in establishing a sustainable, life-enhancing pace. Quiet your mind from its myriad distractions and allow the Holy Spirit to simplify and focus your attention on a "one-thing" life. Awaken your dulled emotions and be motivated by a deep-seated conviction to be real in your relationships, to shun superficiality, and to be "all there" for the people who matter.

These transformations lie at the heart of soulspace, and it is my prayer that throughout this book you will find the tools to help you lay hold of this life.

This tree that charts the operation of the world system is not unlike the tree of the knowledge of good and evil, that notorious plant from which Adam and Eve ate the forbidden fruit. Though Scripture doesn't give us much information about it, this tree symbolizes the system that stands in opposition to God's Kingdom. Its roots are the root sins, its branches are the heart-motivations, and its fruits are the soul clutter of the modern world system. Consider that it was fear (that God was holding out on them), greed (for something more than the abundance they already enjoyed), and pride (that they could evaluate the opportunity better than God) that motivated the first couple toward the first sin. And from the roots of that one action grew up all the branches and fruits of sin that we recognize today in ourselves.

If it were to be diagramed, it might look like this:

Root Sins	Heart-Motivations	Soul Clutter
Fear ————————➤	Insecurity ————————➤	Drivenness
Greed————————➤	Materialism ———————— ➤	Distraction
Pride ————————➤	Control ———————— ➤	Superficiality

Richard Swenson describes soulspace as "margin" and contrasts it with soul clutter in this description of "marginless living":

Marginless is being thirty minutes late to the doctor's office because you were twenty minutes late getting out of the hair-dresser's because you were ten minutes late dropping the children off at school because the car ran out of gas two blocks from the gas station—and you forgot your purse.

Marginless is the baby crying and the phone ringing at the same time; margin is Grandma taking the baby for the afternoon.

Marginless is not having time to finish the book you're reading on stress; margin is having the time to read it twice.[4]

One of the reasons we often manage to live for so long with so much clutter is because of "deferred maintenance." The principle can be illustrated by my family's hotel business, which my grandfather started from nearly nothing. Under first my uncle's leadership and now my cousin's, one Days Inn hotel has grown to more than a dozen extended-stay properties. When the World Trade Center attacks took the economy into a nosedive, one of the money-saving options discussed for these hotel properties was deferred maintenance—temporarily putting off the painting and new carpets and other upkeep items that cost money—until cash flow improved. This approach does work; it does save money—in the short run. But if the hotels were operated in that mode for years instead of months, we would quickly become the proud owners of Roach City. Peeling paint and stained carpets do not produce a healthy hotel business.

Yet many intelligent, well-meaning folks (that means you and me) do exactly that in our own lives. We keep deferring maintenance on the important things—things like getaway weekends with our spouses, "dates" with our daughters, afternoons in personal solitude, or plane trips to see our brothers in other states . . . and then we wonder why those things start to break and fall apart. Of course, it's not the *things*, it's the *people* and the relationships that bind them together that break and fall apart. Long-term deferred maintenance is the philosophy of clutter.

So how about it? Are you a professional procrastinator in nurturing your relationships? Are your to-do lists more compelling than maintaining your soul, your friendships, and your family? If so—and if you have gotten this far in reading this book—then you're probably starting to acknowledge that you have a deep vein of unhappiness throbbing inside yourself. It's there because of the disconnect. Because of the inner tension between your heart's longings and your actual lifestyle. But it doesn't have to be that way. Today, this moment, you can refocus your attention on what really matters! You can make room for God to break in.

In case I'm getting a little too close for comfort, let me take the opportunity here to differentiate between soul clutter and soul sickness (which we'll consider in more detail in chapter 6). These terms are not clinical, of course; they're simply practical ways of associating ideas related to the soul. In broad strokes, soul clutter is the mass of activities generated outside ourselves that we invite inside—only to find it choking the life out of our souls, much like the weeds overwhelmed the good seed in the parable of the sower (see Matthew 13:1–23). In contrast, soul sickness is generated internally, frequently through damage received from another person; it skews our perception of reality, making us susceptible to and reinforcing the clutter in our lives. Soul clutter is more related to our *doing* while soul sickness is more related to our *being*. Because of that difference, clutter is more readily cured than sickness is, yet both must yield to the soul-healing power of our heavenly Father! Both problems keep us from having space in our lives. Both rob us of the life for which we were fashioned.

The truth is that we all experience a level of both soul clutter and soul sickness, so it's not a matter of *whether* we wrestle with these issues but of how much they rule within us. Until we recognize how far we have fallen from grace, we will be powerless to re-obtain it. "It is for freedom," Paul declared, "that Christ has set us free" (Galatians 5:1). Paul lived out this inner reality regardless of whether he was preaching to thousands or alone in prison! This reality is the ultimate aim of soulspace: *soul freedom*. It

> *Freedom is the defining mark of the Kingdom of God.*

is the defining mark of the Kingdom of God, which means that the measure of freedom we live in becomes the gauge measuring our experience of and participation in this Kingdom. "Stand firm, then, and do not let yourselves be burdened again by a yoke of slavery," Paul continued. Having tasted the sweetness of this freedom of soul, why would we ever go back to slavery?

KINGDOM CROSSFIRE

One of the foundational convictions in this book is that the quest and battle for soulspace are parts of the larger war between two realms: the Kingdom of God versus what we are calling the world system. There is a continuous unseen clash between the goals and motivations of heaven and those of hell. Fortunately, God has given us many glimpses into the principles by which His Kingdom operates; some of the greatest ones are found in the Kingdom parables of Matthew 13.

The Sower and the Seed (vv. 3–23)

The parable: A farmer scatters seed (Jesus' message) that falls upon one of four soils—the hard path (stolen by the devil), the rocky soil (dries up with the first sign of trouble), the thorny soil (choked out by weeds of worry and greed), or the good soil (where it takes root and produces a great harvest).

The point: If we want to experience Kingdom treasure in our lives, then we must earnestly cultivate the "soil" of our souls, rooting out soul clutter and soul sickness and applying Kingdom realities from the Word of God.

The Weeds (vv. 24–30)

The parable: After a man plants seed in his field, an enemy sows weeds among the grain. Rather than attempt to uproot the weeds during growth, the farmer decides to wait until harvest and then separate and burn the weeds.

The point: The things of the Kingdom and the things of this world system live intermingled around us, but time will tell where the true value lies.

The Mustard Seed and Yeast (vv. 31–33)

The parable: The mustard seed is the smallest seed but grows into the largest tree. Likewise, yeast is very small but affects a large amount of dough.

The point: That which has greatest heavenly power, and therefore is most important in this world, may initially appear insignificant.

The Hidden Treasure and the Pearl (vv. 44–46)

The parable: When a man discovered a treasure hidden in a field, he sold everything he had to buy the field. Similarly, when a merchant found the most valuable pearl, he sold everything and bought the pearl.

The point: The treasures of the Kingdom require a search; when found, their surpassing worth makes everything else we have seem insignificant.

The Net (vv. 47–50)

The parable: The fisherman's net brings up all kinds of fish, but after the fish are brought to shore, the good ones are separated from the bad.

The point: The confused jumble of valuable and worthless distractions that makes up our world will eventually be discerned and separated.

Jesus saw what was hidden and who was willing to search it out. He knew there were folks who would be seen as foolish in the eyes of the world as they lay hold of that precious Pearl (which represented Christ) and that there were others who would say, "That's interesting," and walk away—away from the Treasure of a lifetime! It's all summed up in the appeal He issued repeatedly: "He who has ears, let him hear" (Matthew 13:9, 43; see also vv. 15–16). That cry still echoes through our world today . . . and our destiny hangs upon it.

How about it? Do you sense something calling to you—a beckoning to live another way? A call to space? The urge you feel is the Holy Spirit, reaching through the window of your heart.

THE WINDOW TO THE SPIRIT

There's an old saying that the eye is the window to the soul. Jesus Himself said that "the eye is the lamp of the body" (Matthew 6:22). Frequently, we can look into someone's eyes and see something of the state of his or her soul.

In a similar way, the soul contains a window to the spirit, a "soul eye," as it were, that perceives the spiritual world either dimly or acutely. As we know, every person has a spirit, and when Christ awakens men and women to their need for a Savior and they embrace Him as Lord, His Spirit moves in and takes up residence, bringing their dead spirits to life! Many, many scriptures talk about this awesome awakening of the human spirit and about the deposit God continues to make within it. Here are a few of them.

Ephesians 2:4–5: But because of his great love for us, God, who is rich in mercy, made us alive with Christ even when we were dead in transgressions.

Romans 8:10: But if Christ is in you . . . your spirit is alive because of righteousness.

Romans 8:15–16: You received the Spirit of sonship. . . . The Spirit himself testifies with our spirit that we are God's children.

So it is within our spirits (small *s*), as distinct from our souls, that the Spirit (big *S*) comes to live. Our spirits have direct communion with God's Spirit as we cultivate the spiritual life. This means that when we pray, when we worship, or when we read the Scriptures, this part of our being is encouraged and lifted up. Whether or not our minds are engaged, our spirits confirm the presence and work of the Holy Spirit and are—to use the biblical term—"edified."

This is an extremely vital thing: the building up of our spirits. Here in our spirits is where we "hear" the voice of God. This is where we discern things on the spiritual level. For example, you walk into a place of business and, for no natural or observable

reason, you "feel" an oppression there or you sense a particular operation of evil . . . or the operation of good, for that matter. This is
clearly not the result of one of your five physical senses, and possibly
it's not an emotional response; it is, in fact, a spiritual sense.

But what is sensed in your spirit must then show up as something
you "feel" in your soul in order to be consciously perceived. Perhaps
this spiritual sense manifests in your emotions as a sudden feeling of
depression. Or it may even affect you physically, let's say by the hair
on your neck suddenly standing up for no explainable reason. As an
example, my college buddy Bill and I took a post-graduation road
trip along the East Coast, beach-hopping with a windsurfer board
strapped to the top of our car. One evening, after scuba diving along
a beautiful stretch of the coast, we decided to drive down to a nearby
beach town and have dinner. As we drove into town, I was overwhelmed with physical sickness. After cruising the city for about fif-
teen minutes and continuing to feel worse and worse, I finally
persuaded Bill that there was some kind of spiritual darkness there
that I couldn't bear. We left . . . and I gradually felt better.

How connected is your spirit to your soul? Do you frequently
sense heaven influencing your thinking and feeling? Remember:
Your soul contains a window to your spirit. Those who understand
this concept and cultivate a life of space have a large, uncluttered
window that connects spiritual realities to their soul senses.
Conversely, those who live life on the gerbil wheel have a shrunken,
atrophied window to the spirit and so cannot perceive accurately
what is taking place in God's realm.

The process itself is transparent; we are not aware of the transaction, but through this window we learn to recognize what is
taking place in the spirit by what we feel, think, and will. And what

is taking place in this realm is the most real—much more real than what we perceive in the physical world.

> *We access spiritual realities through a healthy soul.*

There are two worlds operating, one on top of the other: the natural world and the spiritual world. This is the cosmic understanding behind all of Scripture, and our experience confirms it. You don't have to be a Christian to understand it; many observant and thoughtful people recognize this reality. Because of this, and knowing that the Holy Spirit's job description is to "teach you all things" (John 14:26), we as Christians are motivated to get in tune with the spiritual realities around us.

My point is that we access these spiritual realities through healthy souls—wide and uncluttered windows to our spirits. These spiritual truths show up and register in our minds, or move our emotions, or motivate our wills. A sick soul or a distracted soul will not be able to hear and see what the Holy Spirit wants to communicate. If we believe this, then it makes sense that unless we cultivate and care for this holy part of our beings—the soul—then we will miss the purposes of God for our lives. More than that, we will miss God Himself and throw away His most precious gift to us: the privilege of intimacy with Him and with other image-bearers, those He has brought alongside us to walk this journey with us.

As Kellie and I journeyed through the months following my May 1999 sabbatical, I felt a raging thirst for the life of the Spirit. But I was still trying to drink through a swizzle stick. My soul was in such disarray that the window was almost closed, and the riches of heaven were just out of reach. Our move to Colorado was not the end of that trauma. And, in the words of Winston Churchill, "it [was] not even the beginning of the end. But it [was], perhaps, the end of the beginning."[5]

SOULSPACE PRESCRIPTION

Sit down with your spouse or a close friend over a cup of coffee and ask him or her to tell you with great honesty what level of drivenness, distraction, and superficiality he or she observes in your life. C'mon, you can do it!

chapter four

Breaking into
the Closet

My soul thirsts for God, for the living God. When can I go and
meet with God?

—PSALM 42:2

I HAD BEEN ON THE CHURCH'S STAFF as worship pastor for
about eight years when a good friend came up to me and said
God had given her a "word" for me, but she hoped I wouldn't be
offended by it.

Well, that caught me off guard a bit; it's not what you wake up
every morning wishing to hear! So, with some trepidation, I asked
what God was saying to her. And it was this: God had said to her,
"I have much to say to Jerome, but he isn't always listening."

That's it?! Uh . . . what do you mean, I'm not listening? I thought.
*Don't I have my morning devotions . . . most of the time? Don't I lead
worship and preach? Don't I lead small groups and help strategize the
church's direction? Don't I run a school of worship and teach other leaders
how to hear God?*

But in my heart I knew it was true. I knew that my disciplines
were more often duties than delights, things to be checked off so that

I could get on to the "real work" of the day. Knowing in my depths that I needed more "feet time with Mary"—just being with Jesus—I tried mightily to work out various schemes to accomplish this. For a while I tried taking five minutes at the top of every hour to pray. Then I tried taking the first and last thirty minutes of my workday to be with God. Next I tried taking an hour a day after lunch for worship and prayer. Nothing seemed to stick. And although I enjoyed some of those moments, they still seemed—much to my frustration—to be birthed out of principle rather than true passion for God.

I had marginally better success at scheduling a day of prayer each month. When I took a whole day to be with God, it was wonderfully refreshing and I wondered why I didn't do it more often. But, of course, there was so much to be done. Far from the rose-tinged images some have of full-time ministry, most pastors labor under an often-harsh reality of pressure and expectation. Anytime you see statistics on "job satisfaction" for pastors, you find that an overwhelming number of them want to quit. This is a grievous reality for those who have laid down promising careers and financial security to serve the church. (Because of our own experience with ministry pressures, Kellie and I have a special burden for these precious men and women of God in ministry, which I will discuss in greater detail in chapter 11.)

As much as I enjoyed my job as a worship pastor, this word from God began a gradual, several-year-long awakening to my spiritual poverty of soul. At this time, discipline was more my foe than my friend, leading me repeatedly to condemnation, occasionally to legalism, and frequently to frustration. In the midst of this, Kellie was periodically encouraging me (or nagging me, depending upon my perspective) to spend more time "in the closet," as she called it. She intuitively felt my own spiritual shallowness and knew I needed to deepen my spiritual well so that I could feed others, my family, and myself. I would usually point to whatever feeble attempts I was making at the time, along with my job demands, as my defense. She would drop the subject for a month and then casually and bravely broach it again. I thank God constantly for a wife who has such a burning vision for my spiritual health and doesn't give up on me!

At this point, remembering that struggle in my own life, let me ask you something: Are you resisting the forces pulling at you that just might be the Lord, softly but insistently tugging at your mind? When you are locked into certain ruts and patterns, you may subconsciously shun anything that threatens the status quo—even God Himself! Think about it.

It was probably two years later that a traveling prophet visited our church and called the pastors and elders to the front. After speaking some exciting insights over several of the men, he came to me and made a simple statement. It probably seemed anticlimactic to the congregation, coming as it did after the other stirring pronouncements. But the prophet's words sent an arrow of enlightenment plunging into my life: "God isn't saying much to me about you," he said slowly, almost as though he were a little puzzled, " . . . except, 'Get in the closet!' What He has for you will come as you're with Him in the closet."

Wow! Some people can take a hint, and others of us seem to need the two-by-four approach. Coupled with Kellie's urgings that I should spend more time "in the closet," the words spoken over me that day finally helped me get the idea that perhaps all my to-do lists were not quite as vital to God's Kingdom as I had presumed.

> *Maybe* what I do
> *for God is not as*
> *important as* who
> I am *for God.*

Maybe . . . just maybe, I realized, *what I do* for God is not as important as *who I am* for God. If "being" is more fundamental in the rules of the Kingdom than "doing," then maybe God is less interested in how much I read the Bible than in how much the Bible reads me! Maybe it's not how many chapters but how many changes. Maybe it's not this Sunday's sermon, but the sermon of my life that He most desires.

SOUL HUNGER

Upon settling in Colorado Springs, one of the first things I did was to begin taking one day each week as a prayer day. I would usually rent a room in the World Prayer Center for five dollars a day and hole up there for six or seven hours. After the novelty and the halo of that first prayer day wore off—after about an hour—I had to face the reality that this was hard work. How do you actually spend extended time with God? I knew that intimacy with the Lord was my greatest goal, but I didn't know how to get there. Gradually, over the months that followed, I learned a few things about progressing toward that goal.

The first thing I learned was that becoming a friend of God takes time. There are no shortcuts. No substitutions. There is something about spending extended time alone with God that allows all the soul clutter to subside, all the clamorings of duty to fade, and all the spiritual senses to wake up. This lesson wasn't learned in one day.

Not even in one month. But as week followed week, I began to learn something about quieting my soul and listening to God. Primarily, I learned that this quieting and listening doesn't happen without a deep, gnawing hunger for God.

Are *you* hungry yet?

What could be more refreshing, more satisfying, than knowing God? Jesus said the greatest commandment (in other words, the greatest opportunity) is to love God (see Mark 12:29–31). But how can we love someone we don't really know? We can perhaps have an altruistic or affectionate sentiment for someone without knowing him, but that's a far cry from love. Rather, the quality and depth of our love directly corresponds to the quality and depth of our relationship.

When a prostitute poured out her tears and priceless perfume on the feet of Jesus in the house of a Pharisee (see Luke 7:36–50), Jesus made an explicit connection between the depth of her forgiveness and the depth of her love. As this woman experienced Jesus' forgiveness she was led into a *relational knowledge* of God that far exceeded all the "book knowledge" of the educated Pharisee. She spent time at the feet of Jesus, not unlike Mary of Bethany, whom we discussed earlier, and that time at His feet became the fountain of her great love.

Time leads to relationship. Relationship produces experiential knowledge. And experiential knowledge brings forth love. You can make a tangible deposit in your fountain of love for God by spending extra time with the Lover of your soul! It's so simple, but it's not at all easy. Yet our hearts yearn for this intimacy, and it lies well within our reach. Let's not be denied this life we long for!

Better Than Chocolate

Kellie describes soul hunger in this insight that grew from a dream: "There have been times in my life when I've been especially desperate for God. But great obstacles of stronghold, fear, and uncertainty have stood in my way. Yet always God has called me to press into Him with determination. Many times His presence has become apparent to me after I sit quietly . . . and wait . . . some-

> *Our hearts yearn for this intimacy, and it lies well within our reach!*

times feeling nothing for an hour or more! And then He suddenly comes and speaks to my heart the very things I most need to hear.

"During this stage of our lives, as we pondered what changes we needed to make, I had been thinking about this way of God and looking up the many Bible verses that talk about seeking and searching. That night I had a dream, and in my dream I was sitting at a round table in a lovely room with lots of flowers. The table was covered with a white linen tablecloth and set with a beautiful tea set. As I sat at this table with my friends, a waiter delivered a large, multitiered dessert tray. Each tier was full of the most luscious-looking pastries and cakes I had ever seen! Immediately my eye was drawn to a chocolate pastry on the first tier; I had only glanced at the other tiers, but this was the only chocolate dessert I saw (and what else is there but chocolate?!), so I grabbed it.

"After I had eaten and enjoyed the pastry, one of my friends asked me if there were any other chocolate desserts on the tray. I said, 'I don't know. Let me look.' Then I began to carefully search through the other tiers of the tray, and I saw loads of beautiful, sumptuous delights. But it wasn't until I reached the last tier and looked deep into the middle of the plate that my eyes bulged. For there, right in the middle and behind the others, I saw it! Its dark-chocolate cream icing was topped with tantalizing chunks of gourmet chocolate; it was a much grander dessert than the one I had eaten. I couldn't help feeling sad that I had eaten the first chocolate pastry I'd found without searching to see if there was something even better.

"God spoke to me through this dream, reminding me there are far greater delights in Him than we can imagine (see Ephesians 3:20), and He beckoned my heart to seek out and pursue these love gifts that He lavishly offers. 'You have tasted good things in Me,' He seemed to say, 'but you can't imagine all that I want to give you!'

"It's true that the *good* is the enemy of the *best,* and I believe that many times I have settled for the good things of God that came easily when all along the best things of God went undiscovered and untasted. We can live a happy, contented life with our families and friends, going to church, working on relationships, serving in different capacities—but still miss the real treasures of God!

"Colossians 2:3 says 'all the treasures of wisdom and knowledge' are hidden in Christ. That tells me I need to go on a treasure hunt! God wants to be sought after! He wants to be treasured enough to become our greatest quest!"

Devotion, Obedience, and the Pleasure of God

If you're like me (Jerome), Kellie's inspired "treasure-hunt" idea sounds substantially different than the well-intentioned admonitions to "make sure you're having your thirty minutes of devotions every day." We need to understand that when it comes to satisfying our soul hunger, *devotions* and *devotion* are not the same thing.

God wants to be treasured enough to become our greatest quest!

A dog can be expertly trained to obey a litany of commands without being devoted to its master, while another dog can be sorely lacking in discipline but absolutely and completely given over to its master's heart. The telling difference is usually found in the master's delight in the dog (or lack of it), combined with the amount of time dog and master spend in one another's presence. Although the heart-connection of devotion is the greater virtue, the combination of devotion and obedience brings the highest potential for companionship and purpose. Not unlike ourselves!

Obedience is the foundation for relationship, but obedience is only the beginning, not the end. Many Christians live their lives within the confines of "because-I-said-so" childishness. While that level of compliance is blessed in a five-year-old, it becomes tragic in the relationship between God and a twenty-five-year-old. Or a forty-five-year-old! Instead, God extends an invitation far beyond the demands of obedience that rightfully calls us to bow before the lordship of our Sovereign.

"Then you will call upon me and come and pray to me, and I will listen to you. You will seek me and find me when you seek me with all your heart. I will be found by you," declares the LORD. (Jeremiah 29:12–14)

God's promise to us through the mouth of Jeremiah is that our wholehearted quest for Him will unfailingly draw Him to us. What kind of a God is this who would make such an offer? And to us, no less!

The biblical metaphors lead us down a road of increasing depth of intimacy with God (the italics are mine):

"No longer a *slave* but a *son*" (Galatians 4:7).

"Instead, I have called you *friends*" (John 15:15).

"The two will become *one flesh*. . . . I am talking about Christ and the church" (Ephesians 5:31–32).

The scriptures' frequent imagery of marital love as the epitome of God's relationship with His people highlights the quality of fellowship He desires with us. It's a fellowship of openness, vulnerability, trust, and delight.

The biblical metaphors lead us down a road of increasing depth of intimacy with God: slave . . . son . . . friends . . . one flesh.

I asked the question before: Why would God make us work and search for Him? My answer is (1) because what we invest ourselves in, we value; (2) because like us, God wants to be wanted; and (3) because it makes Him happy to do it that way! Jesus saw this divine preference in operation and exclaimed, "I praise you, Father, Lord of heaven and earth, because you have hidden these things from the wise and learned, and revealed them to little children. Yes, Father, for this was your good pleasure" (Luke 10:21).

The pleasure of God is a contagious thing. His own great happiness overflows intentionally into our hearts the more we are around Him. John Piper uses a wonderfully provocative expression when he insists that our greatest call in life is to become "Christian hedonists"—pursuers of joy in the treasures of God. In this declaration Piper calls C. S. Lewis to the stand as a witness:

> If we consider the unblushing promises of reward and the staggering nature of the rewards promised in the Gospels, it would seem that our Lord finds our desires not too strong, but too weak. We are half-hearted creatures, fooling about with drink and sex and ambition when infinite joy is offered us, like an ignorant child who wants to go on making mud pies in a slum because he cannot imagine what is meant by the offer of a holiday at the sea. We are far too easily pleased.[1]

SEEKING OUT THE CONCEALER'S TREASURE

Pleasure is a creation of God, and His greatest desire is to lavish it upon us. Yet sometimes He conceals it from us, perhaps because He knows that true delight comes from the *pursuit* of His presence . . . because He Himself is our source. Across thousands of years, His searchers have testified to the Concealer's desire to be sought out, as well as to the satisfaction found in the discovery:

- "If you seek him, he will be found by you" (1 Chronicles 28:9).

- "Hear my voice when I call, O LORD; be merciful to me and answer me. My heart says of you, 'Seek his face!' Your face, LORD, I will seek. Do not hide your face from me, do not turn your servant away in anger; you have been my helper. Do not reject me or forsake me, O God my Savior. Though my father and mother forsake me, the LORD will receive me" (Psalm 27:7–10).

- "The lions may grow weak and hungry, but those who seek the LORD lack no good thing" (Psalm 34:10).

- "O God, you are my God, earnestly I seek you; my soul thirsts for you, my body longs for you, in a dry and weary land where there is no water" (Psalm 63:1).

- "Blessed are they who keep his statutes and seek him with all their heart" (Psalm 119:2).

- "And if you call out for insight and cry aloud for understanding, and if you look for it as for silver and search for it as for hidden treasure, then you will understand the fear of the LORD and find the knowledge of God" (Proverbs 2:3–5).

- "I will get up now and go about the city, through its streets and squares; I will search for the one my heart loves" (Song of Solomon 3:2).

- "But seek first his kingdom and his righteousness, and all these things will be given to you as well" (Matthew 6:33).

- "Ask and it will be given to you; seek and you will find; knock and the door will be opened to you" (Matthew 7:7).

It seems that our quest for God is of great importance to Him; in fact, it seems to lie at the center of our very purpose. Paul stated in Acts 17:27 that "God [created us] so that men would seek him and perhaps reach out for him and find him, though he is not far from each one of us." He earnestly desires that we seek, that we reach, and then He promises we will find.

Psalm 25 uses an enlightening phrase when it says that "the secret of the LORD is for those who fear Him" (v. 14 NASB). You mean God has secrets? You betcha! A secret is meant to be shared, but only among the best of friends. And God says that a life vested in fearing Him (honoring Him, seeking Him) will obtain a rare reward: God will share His secrets with us! What kind of secrets? Well, that's between Him and you (*psst* . . . it's a secret!).

God will share His secrets with us!

Maybe it will be something like the warm blanket of His love that He wrapped around me last week as I caught a glimpse of how pure and strong is His delight in me. When my toddlers were wobbling through the family room at age one, they couldn't express their love for Dad in any words—no poetry, no heartrending lyrics—just a face-splitting smile and chubby arms upraised . . . and Dad melted! God's secret whispered into my ear that day was the flood of delight He loves to lavish on this spiritual child.

Or maybe your secret will come, as it did for me, on that July day in 1996 when I sat in one-hundred-degree North Carolina humidity at a Promise Keepers event and God dropped this sentence into my heart: *Ask Me for a son.* The glad-hearted joy that flooded over me that day was reprised two months later when the pregnancy test came back positive and then another nine months later when I held that beautiful red-faced boy in my hands!

An awesome secret was shared with Simeon two thousand years ago. He and Anna, unique among the many devout Jews of the time, were prophetically moved to anticipate and recognize the baby Jesus as the Messiah (see Luke 2:25–38). Their commitment to seeking God day and night allowed them to hold another beautiful red-faced Boy in their hands!

Another biblical facet of soul search is found in the urgent appeal from Isaiah to "seek the LORD while he may be found; call on him while he is near" (55:6). A sobering reality surfaces between the lines here; it tells us that timing is an issue. The quest that is put off for another day may be lost altogether. The time "while he may be found" and the time "while he is near" will not last forever. Just as none of us wishes to face the opportunity cost of missing our kids' childhood through distraction, neither do we wish to live with the haunting sorrow of a life with God we could have had, if only . . .

How Do You Do Soul Search?

So, assuming that our hearts are set upon the quest, let's get practical. How do you do soul search? In my experience, it's more of an attitude than an outline—more about the desire to connect with God than about a formula. Passion will always fuel the pursuit. Passion will cause you to be always looking for this Person—whether you're reading a book, watching a movie, sitting quietly on a lake dock (as I am right now), or even having devotions.

Read the Bible to hear the whispers of its Author. Pray, not to cover all the needs on your list, but to immerse yourself within the heart of the One who answers prayer. Be creative in your search. Be determined in your search. Pinpoint the thing you'd most like to change in your life and search out everything the Bible has to say about it. Ask God why He says the things He does. Find someone you know who lives in the reality you desire and probe his or her experience. Journal your heart to God . . . and then journal His heart back to you. You will be surprised at what you find.

As I have already alluded to, time is a crucial element of the search. There is a misunderstanding among many that *quality* time is the goal, that *how* you spend time with God is more important than *how long* you spend with Him. My experience is quite the opposite—that extended periods of time with God are far more productive in the relationship than applying this or that method for short bites of time. Of course, as in any relationship, there are all sorts of ways to be in contact with God: from the quickie petition at the stoplight for that meeting we're about to enter . . . to the blessing of gratitude over a meal . . . to the urgent cry for healing of a child's 103-degree temperature. It's all part of a vital, healthy relationship, but if your relationship with God is surviving on five-minute interactions, then it is unquestionably an unmotivated search. And as a result, the Treasure remains hidden in the field for another seeker.

There is no right amount of time to spend with God. But there is a direct correlation between time spent and passion for the quest. It's not rocket science. And it's not always the early bird who gets the worm; it's the hungry bird! The bird that won't quit until it has satiated its hunger.

Facing the Dragon

We cannot discuss the quest for God without bringing attention to the fact that there is a very real adversary to the search. Satan hates your quest more than just about anything, and he uses his greatest efforts to hinder you. He and his spiritual cronies will personally see to it that when you embark on the search, you will be harangued by interruptions, worries, accusations, and frustrations. Chief on his list are busyness, distrac-

> *Satan hates your quest more than just about anything!*

tion, and discouragement. When (not if) these things occur, you will have a choice to make: Will you succumb to the dragon's eye-burning smoke and bail out of the search, or will you strengthen your resolve to lay hold of the goal?

Just last week when I had set aside a prayer day, I sat down to focus upon the search at hand. As I began to lay bare my thoughts on the journal page, I found myself writing these words:

> Even now there is this insistent voice in my head that says, "God's not going to talk to you. Why should He talk to you? Anyway, it's too much work to try to hear Him. You're going to spend all day trying to convince God to say something and if you're lucky, you'll get a word or two. A couple lines maybe from a whole day of listening . . . not much to show for a day of prayer!"

Honestly, I had no idea all that crud was being whispered into my ear. All I knew on the conscious level was that I should be excited about this great day of opportunity. Instead, my soul felt nonchalant, even indifferent. This is the "third voice," as John Eldredge calls it, that every one of us regularly hears . . . but doesn't usually notice. We "hear" it on an emotional level without processing it through our minds to understand where it's coming from. Fortunately, we can also hear the voice of the divine Quest Guide calling us quietly but determinedly to the search (see John 10:27). We must train ourselves to recognize the voices we hear and decide whom to listen to—the Shepherd or the dragon?

Unfortunately, this dragon has an accomplice who speaks from an unexpected platform: our own hearts! Yes, there is a traitorous part of ourselves that we must also engage and vanquish repeatedly on the quest. It goes by many names—the flesh, the Old Man, the sinful nature, the dark side, etc. Whatever you call it, it is a daily reality, and its methods are many. Primarily, this inner foe keeps us oriented on ourselves: our comfort, our material wants, our entertainment. Or conversely, it drives us fervently forward on other, less meaningful quests: perhaps an all-consuming job, perhaps other addictions.

In the pages that follow, we will journey together into the freedom of soul God has prepared for us. We will look into our own experiences and find the soul sickness and soul clutter that dull our hearts and keep us shut off from God. And together we will chart a course to space—space in our families, space in our work, and space in our very souls. Where God breaks in.

SOULSPACE PRESCRIPTION

Ask yourself this question: What has God spoken to me this week, and how has it changed me?

If you can't answer this question, what does that say about the condition of your quest?

chapter five

"With a Big Sky Over Me"

Let people feel the weight of who you are . . . and let them deal
with it.

—BRENT CURTIS

IDENTITY. WHAT AN ELUSIVE CONCEPT! I woke up a few weeks ago
with a dream clutching stubbornly at my mind—one of those
frustrating sequences where everything goes wrong and you can't
quite do what you're supposed to do. In my case, I was supposed to
be leading worship, but . . . I was late. Then my guitar strap broke. I
was out of tune. And I couldn't think of any songs to play. My heart
was racing with tension, and I felt all eyes weighing upon me!
Waking did not relieve the heaviness upon my soul. But interestingly,
as I awoke, I heard a song playing in my head, a phrase of a song
actually: ". . . somewhere in Montana with a big sky over me."[1]

I recognized it from a cowboy song on a CD my girls had been
playing recently. But as that phrase played back through my mind in
those early moments of awakening, with my dream still fresh in the
background, the words took on an almost transcendent quality within
me: The "big sky" seemed to capture an emotion, a longing for some

kind of freedom. Yes . . . a freedom from fear . . . the fear of failure. The image of that cowboy strumming his guitar around the campfire and reveling in his big sky all at once became my own. It became my own anthem of liberty from a performance-based life. A liberation from living underneath the crush of other people's expectations—maybe even my own!

"Big Sky" freedom comes directly from knowing who you are.

Later that day, I went back to read the lyrics of the song more carefully and found some intriguing elements. Although the tune is punctuated with complaints of hard riding and stale biscuits, the underlying joy of those "free-riding rovers" seeps through. Yet it was something else that leapt off the page at me, from the last line of the second verse: a clear, bold statement of identity. "Born to be a cowboy, and I guess I'll never change!" Born for something. Danged if that cowboy hadn't figured out who he was! As a deep sigh escaped me, I wished I were as lucky. But one penetrating idea was taking shape in my mind: Big-sky freedom, I mused, comes directly from knowing who you really are—from enjoying that defining sense of purpose that grips the soul with confidence and ushers you forward into life with wide-eyed anticipation.

CLUES OF CLARITY . . . FROM THE COWBOY

But where does this clarity of purpose and identity come from? As a Christian, my first response is to answer, "Well, from God of course." Yes . . . but how to lay hold of it—that is the question! Are there any clues from the cowboy? I studied the song again, hunting for any hidden nuggets of revelation from this saddle-bound philosopher. Three facts from these lines of verse seemed to bear significance: (1) the cowboy is anchored in his past, (2) he is drawn into his future by love, and (3) he is confirmed in his calling by his comrades.

Blast from the Past

That first fall in Colorado, as I began to unpack my baggage and lay out my mess before the Lord, I felt like the October aspen tree out back—losing my glorious coat of gold and left with bare, ugly branches. The brownness of the landscape mirrored the barrenness of my own self-understanding as I had to acknowledge that I had been playing out a part, reading off a script compiled from unstudied assumptions, idealized role models, and some mysterious elements of my true self. But the problem was that I didn't know which was which!

This discovery is part of the journey of the soul that most people rarely seem to get to. We just keep moving along, day after day, rarely questioning our direction and purpose as long as things don't get too uncomfortable. Life has a way of setting its own agenda, and it takes the intentional and forceful creation of space to begin to ask—and answer—these all-important questions.

There are, of course, the expected answers. First, *the practical answers:* I am a single mom, struggling to make ends meet; I don't have the luxury of wrangling with such esoteric questions. I am a businessman, a husband, and a father; I'm just doing the best I can to provide for my family. I am a single woman, and until I get married, I have no compelling sense of purpose; but I try to drown that lack of direction by immersing myself in my work.

And then there are *the religious answers:* I exist to bring glory to God. My identity is a blood-washed, Spirit-filled, devil-overcoming soldier of the cross.

Okay . . . these phrases contain some great and powerful truths, but how deeply do they penetrate your own soul with revelation? How do they define you in the daily grind? Until theology is personalized in soul transaction—you and God in the muddy trenches of life—it remains a cerebral exercise, empty of any defining power toward identity, powerless to draw us to God Himself.

How does the past shape our present identities?

This roundabout route takes me to my first question: How does the past shape our present identities?

Our cowboy friend makes telling reference to riding on "grandpa's saddle" and carrying his "daddy's six-gun." Apparently, he is a third-generation trail-rider, and this heritage has influenced his own set of goals and priorities. But maybe the question is not so much "How does our past shape us?" as it is "How *should* our past shape us?" Or perhaps, "How should it *not* shape us?"

Home Improvement. As parents, we are entrusted with the rather large undertaking of crafting our children's emerging identities—their first sense of self and their sense of family. Their foundations of right and wrong. Their understanding of God, His world, and their place in it. As parents, we succeed, and we fail; we cry bitter tears, and then we stare in grateful amazement; we pray, and we hope. Scripture is interwoven with explicit commands and implicit (better and worse) examples for parents to impart to their children a heritage, a family-specific history of the ways and works of God. As parents, we walk a fine line between implanting the discoveries of our own souls and nurturing our children's own self-discovery of soul.

As children, we have no say in the heritage granted us—the good, the bad, and the ugly we receive and sort through and try to make sense of. And then, in those early teenage years, we begin to build the kind of person we want to become. Drawing from family models, idols and heroes, what's "in" and "cool" at school this week, and vague hints of an inner self, we start to subconsciously construct an identity. Growing up in the church, I witnessed many young men and women awakening somewhere between age twelve and fourteen and grappling, struggling like butterflies to extricate themselves from their cocoons and wondering what they were becoming. They began to examine, as I did, the things they had been taught, and then they sought to find if those ideas resonated in harmony or dissonance with their own souls. Some embraced their heritage; others disavowed it. But either way, heritage is heritage. It is what it is.

Many years later some of us awaken again, usually due to a crisis of some sort, to wonder how it is we became this . . . this person. And we begin to wonder what parts of us are real, what makes them real, and how we become more real.

You've Got Mail. In the movie *You've Got Mail,* Tom Hanks's character stands in line at his local coffee shop and quips as he watches in amazement a string of young, hip dot-commers order their double-tall-decaf-skinny-dry-caramel-macchiatos, "The whole purpose of places like Starbucks is for people who have no decision-making ability whatsoever to make six decisions just to buy one cup of coffee. . . . So people who don't know . . . who on earth they are can, for only two dollars and ninety-five cents, get not just a cup of coffee but an absolutely defining sense of self."

One hopes this is not the high-water mark for contemporary identity, but it's not until we begin the fearsome process of self-examination that we can be sure we are not equally superficial. "A defining sense of self" is an essential commodity for the journey of the soul, yet clearly this self-knowledge is not derived from our taste in coffee but from studied inquiry into our natural and supernatural formation. Scripture states that both God and humans work together to affect history (see 1 Corinthians 3:9 and 2 Corinthians 6:1), and the formation of a soul is no exception. The people and forces in our past are some of the strongest shaping dynamics we experience.

> *Self-knowledge is derived from studied inquiry into our natural and supernatural formation.*

As a child, my parents made large and frequent deposits of love and truth into my soul. This had an enormous grounding effect upon my security and the subsequent relationship that grew among us. This stood in stark contrast to the alienation I experienced among my peers in high school, where I was a hopeless misfit. I have a vivid recollection of sitting in Mrs. Henderson's algebra II class beside Joe Jock, who disdainfully asked me why I was wearing blue socks with my tennis shoes instead of the requisite white. I had no satisfactory answer, reinforcing my assignment to what I call the "out-caste." One's identity quivers from the blow.

These powerful forces drove me to God and to my family but away from the world to discover my identity. This was mostly good in that the isolation kept me from some of the more damaging misdirections of my contemporaries, but it also defined my soul largely by the pursuit of safety and stunted the growth of my emerging strength as a man. I can see now that many of the crises and threats of those formative years were met by passivity instead of courage, by withdrawal instead of engagement. So twenty years later, as I waded through the debris of my soul in wintry Colorado, I began to see the roots of my false self and began to yearn for the restoration of my lost manhood.

The past, then, shapes us mightily, but it remains for us to discern what parts of that shaping are true and what parts are false, based upon our understanding of God's blueprint for the "real me." Some people are enormously damaged in their early years through abuse or tragedy, yet the power of God for redemption is limitless in the recovery of our true selves. While I began to seek God for the recovery of my masculine strength, I noted in both my father and my father's father a bold, adventuresome spirit that I began to claim as my own. So, my cowboy friend, I too ride upon my "grandpa's saddle" and carry my "daddy's six-gun." I am anchored in my heritage—but I have a new trail to ride, my own personalized mission that is not theirs but mine.

Back to the Future

My next observation of the cowboy is that he is drawn into his future by love—by a passion that is uniquely his own. In the song, that passion is his sweetheart who is awaiting his return back home. This passion takes us to the inner sense of calling that resides in each one of us but often requires diligent seeking to unearth.

The cowboy is drawn into his future by a passion that is uniquely his own.

There are those rare few whose destiny grabs them early on and from grade school possesses them with an unswerving aim to become that doctor or firefighter or what have you.

I got a whiff of my future in the summer following my sleepover saga, recounted in chapter 2. In the unhurried hours of those summer mornings, I found the Scriptures coming alive as I read them, and for the first time, they seemed to overflow with God's customized wisdom for my life. I couldn't get enough! And one morning in those precious moments of newfound intimacy with my Father, I heard Him speak deeply into my soul. This time it came as a question: *Would anything else in life be more satisfying and meaningful than full-time ministry?* With that simple, rather innocuous question came an excitement and a deep stirring that gripped my imagination. It wasn't preaching per se that captivated me but just a hunger to know God and help other people know Him. I remember going with a cautiously optimistic anticipation into the kitchen to tell my mom what had happened.

Although that vision never faltered, I had no clear picture of how and where this journey would take me. My love for worship was the strongest signal on my compass, so I followed it through Bible college, business school, and seminary until I found myself the worship pastor in my father's church. My passion for worshiping God was strong enough to carry me for ten years in that position, but I also discovered that a job has the power to obscure a calling, even if the two are similar. It was that realization that confirmed my departure from that position.

In October 2000, I sat down to try to put pen to paper regarding my identity and my calling. Our Colorado pastor had been speaking recently on the power of a personal purpose statement, and I had crafted various versions over the years. But as I set about it this time,

I knew it would be different—that the parameters of life that had kept my prior self safe within its box were now gone! So I sat.

And I sat.

The blank sheet of paper before me mocked my uncertainty. After long minutes, I laid it aside and walked away. Days later, I asked myself a less threatening question: *If I could do anything in the world, without limitation, what would I do? What was it in my past experiences that brought me greatest joy and satisfaction?*

Hmmm . . . I paused, mentally touching those times and places in worship when my entire being had been transfixed by the nearness of God, not wanting to move a muscle for fear of losing the precious delicacy of that moment . . . remembering the thrill of connecting with a person, or a crowd of people, by sharing my experience with God in a way that had ignited and focused their hunger for Him . . . recalling the contentment and renewal of soul I found in the pine-scented, fog-laced mountains of North Carolina. Yes, there were fragments of purpose here.

Real and Supernatural. As we became familiar with our Colorado setting over the ensuing weeks, I pondered these questions, and one day I heard God speak into my heart with a defining word: *You are called to be real and to be supernatural.* And I knew what He meant. "Realness" was a call to honesty and transparency; it was a call to know myself and to know others in a way that confronted superficiality and religiosity. It was a call to live what I believed and to gamble upon a dream. As a firstborn, I had embodied the characteristics of responsibility and caution. But now I knew that the wildness that had driven us sixteen hundred miles from home was not a fluke but rather a holy calling to a God-intoxicated recklessness.

And *supernatural*? As I reflected over my past years of life and ministry, I began to grieve the sheer "naturalness" of it all. I saw in myself a great fear of putting myself in situations where I would be utterly dependent upon God, an unwillingness to go out on a limb in my worship leading. *Just stick to the song list,* my mind would tell me. *Don't take risks; you might crash and burn.* Programming in church services feels like a double-edged sword.

The wildness that had driven us sixteen hundred miles from home was not a fluke but rather a holy calling to a God-intoxicated recklessness.

Let me give you a little window into the planning that often goes on behind the scenes for church services. You have a certain amount of time for a Sunday morning service (if you are running multiple services, those boundaries become more rigid). You want to accomplish certain things—for instance, worship, communion, announcements, a song from the children's ministry, a sermon, and maybe time for prayer and personal ministry. Frequently, each agenda item gets allotted a certain number of minutes in order to fit in everything that seems important. That kind of planning brings intentionality and a certain amount of safety from disorder. But it can easily reflect our human agenda at the expense of God's intentions. What if it's God who wants to break into our order?

I began to feel that many times I had programmed God's wildness out of my agenda. In my desire to keep worship services flowing smoothly and without disruption, it felt safer to stick to the program instead of risking God's supernatural interventions. It is now my deep desire to be moved completely by the Spirit of God, even if it's not so neat and tidy.

I'm not sure who started all the talk about God's being "a gentleman," but I think it is misleading. That we can trust Him to be utterly good and kind in our lives is without question; however, the term *gentleman* conjures up notions of politeness . . . no surprises . . . no disruptions . . . no inconvenience. Hogwash! God is eminently unpredictable and wild. In C. S. Lewis's inimitable words, "He's not a tame lion!"[2]

I'm not sure who started all this talk about God being a "gentleman," but I think it is misleading.

I want to be a part of events where everyone knows that God showed up! I have no desire to do ministry that can be accomplished without the active engagement of God's power and grace. In fact, if there's one word I hope to hear at the end of my life and ministry, it's that word I felt God speaking into my heart: *supernatural.* I don't mean I have visions of stepping into a phone booth and changing from an everyday preacher to a cape-clad superhero. To be supernatural means I want to be a man of humility, because this mentality will inevitably bring messes—places and times where I will look foolish, where "the show didn't happen." But that's where I have to be humble and real about what and who I am . . . and what I'm not. Who really cares what Jerome thinks? Will that change the world? I think not. But when the supernatural life of Jesus is flowing through Jerome's words and songs and actions—well, that's something worth being a part of! That is a world-changing force! My prayer is that every day this reality would be true of me . . . and of you!

And so my life began to focus on a passion that was drawing me into a specific future. Finally I realized, *This is what I am made for. This is part of the true me.*

Just like my cowboy friend.

O Brother, Where Art Thou?

Number three on the cowboy's list of identity-shapers is his comrades' confirming influence upon his calling. He's not riding alone. He is surrounded by men who have the same general vision and purpose he does; together they form a community united by a common goal and shared experience. Good and bad—they're in it together. That unity is something we all crave; we all yearn to know that we are not alone but that we are part of something bigger than ourselves.

We'll talk more about the importance of *community* in chapter 8. But for now let me say this: Community is more than just the social expression of our human need for fellowship. It has everything to do with identity. When our foundation from the past meets our passion for the future and the resulting purpose resounds within a group of like-minded men or women, our souls become fully alive and we engage life as our true selves. This is a holy and awesome thing and actually incarnates the prayer of Christ to the Father that "your kingdom come, your will be done on earth as it is in heaven"! Gil Bailie said, "Don't ask yourself what the world needs. Ask yourself what makes you come alive . . . because what the world needs is people who have come alive!"[3] The Kingdom of God and the love of God invade planet earth through such people. These people know who they are. They know their God. And that is an unstoppable combination!

WHO IS SEARCHING WHOM?

The search for our own hearts and the search for God are not really different searches. God already knows us, but *we* don't know us. So we have this urgent need to know ourselves with God's true perspective. As King David expressed so beautifully, "Search me, O God, and know my heart; test me and know my anxious thoughts. See if there is any offensive way in me and lead me in the way everlasting" (Psalm 139:23–24). The more we peer into the heart of God, the more we see the reflection of our own hearts looking back at us!

The Word of God—both written and spoken—is a mirror (see James 1:23). When we see ourselves by divine revelation, we have the opportunity to take that word into ourselves, act on it, and be transformed by the power of it. God's truth is designed to be the agent of change, blessing, and freedom (see v. 25).

The search for God and the search for self are deeply intertwined. An insight into one almost always leads us to insight into the other. For example, consider the advice in James 1:22: "Do not merely listen to the word, and so deceive yourselves. Do what it says."

> *The search for God and the search for self are deeply intertwined.*

What does that passage say about our hearts? It says, in James's wonderful, no-nonsense style, that we have a tremendous capacity as humans to live in denial—to agree with truth in the abstract but to allow pride, busyness, or apathy to completely rob that truth of its life-changing potency in our lives through our own neglect.

Ouch! James is really getting in our faces. But if we open our souls to that word, we can feel its power softening our hearts and drawing us closer to our God.

Now, what does that reveal to us about God? It tells us several wonderful things about Him: First, it says that God gives us a certain amount of freedom within the realm of the soul to receive or reject His Word, to pursue freedom or to let it pass us by. Second, it reflects God's desires for the fellowship that comes through our agreeing with His Word. Because if we agree with the words from His mouth and let them transform us, they will draw us into a whole new level of intimacy with Him. Third, this verse calls us to change—with an implicit promise that He will make that change possible! So to summarize, this one verse, which on its face speaks to us about ourselves, also leads us to a God who (1) holds us responsible, (2) earnestly desires our fellowship, and (3) gives us the power to change. It's true: The search for God and the search for self are deeply intertwined!

A Holy Wrestling Match

Growing up, my respect for God made me strongly reluctant to question Him. *If I don't understand something,* I reasoned, *then God is right, I am wrong, and maybe someday I'll understand it.* That attitude is true as far as it goes, but it fails to take into account that God, strangely, *invites* us to wrestle with Him!

I came across a passage related to this idea recently in Gordon Dalbey's book *Healing the Masculine Soul.* In it Dalbey recalled,

Years ago, when I taught at an inner-city junior high school, I came upon an angry scene in which one boy was challenging another to a fight. "He's calling you out!" others yelled to the one challenged. What if the essential nature of manhood is revealed as our Creator God "calls us out," even to frightening occasions of conflict, challenge, and risk—even to struggle against Himself, and His desires for us?[4]

I was stunned. Dalbey seemed to dangerously imply that sometimes God picks a fight with us. Could that be true? This thought was troubling on several counts: First, if God were to fight with me, wouldn't He be luring me into something inherently wrong—contending with the Almighty? Second, wouldn't this be a rather one-sided affair and put me at extreme risk?

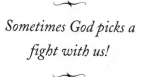

Sometimes God picks a fight with us!

And third, what possible good could come of such an encounter?

As I pondered this mind-bending possibility, my thoughts drifted to several biblical accounts that confirm the truth of it. David the Psalmist seemed to take extraordinary freedoms in his laments. If you cut through the Bibletalk, it is obvious that David engaged in monumental whining. He complained up one side and down the other. He regularly challenged God's justice, God's attentiveness, God's compassion, and God's timing! What's up with that?! How did he get away with all that and still have such intimacy as to be called the "man after God's own heart"?

Apparently, there is complaining . . . and then there's *complaining*. I think the difference is, there is complaining with pride and complaining with humility. God seems to allow great liberties for those who are absolutely abandoned to Him, whereas He is quick to judge those who rise up with a haughty spirit. Not only does He allow those who know Him well to wrestle with Him, but He seems to actually invite them into the contest.

Enter Jacob. Enter Angel of God. Jacob and Angel wrestle. Jacob goes away with a blessing. Jacob also goes away limping.

This story, told in Genesis 32:24–32, is truly startling. If you are very familiar with it, it may have lost its shock value for you. But look again . . . God initiates this contest with Jacob right when Jacob is teetering on the edge of both his destiny and his identity. Up until this point, his life has been one long struggle: two steps forward, one and a half steps back. Although God has blessed and protected him, Jacob has yet to carve out a life for himself and his family. He has had one significant encounter with God at Bethel many years prior to this wrestling match, but he still has not come to terms with who he is in the divine plan.

Interestingly, all of my concerns about "fighting" with God are addressed in this account of Jacob in Genesis 32. First, it shows that God does not seem to think our wrestling with Him is a bad thing; the bout with Jacob was God's idea. Second, I am definitely at risk. No question about it. However, the risk of being injured by God is preferable to the risk of being injured by my own foolishness; God's "injuries" are redemptive, while the injuries I generate are destructive. Third, Jacob's rounds with God were the best thing that ever happened to him. Let's take a closer look at why that was so.

When God is finished with him, Jacob has obtained three things of tremendous value: a name, a blessing, and a limp. His new name, *Israel*, means "he struggles with God" and, far from being an accusation, it is now his banner. It is his claim to intimacy; you can't wrestle without getting very, very close—skin on skin. In getting closer to God, Jacob has discovered his own true identity—a pursuer of the face of God—and it shapes the rest of his life. The blessing he receives is not defined in these verses, but it is sufficient to know that God communicated His favor upon Jacob and released him into the destiny of leading a nation, a nation that bears his name and his calling to "[struggle] with God and men and . . . overcome" (Genesis 32:28). Finally, there's Jacob's limp. It is tangible, unforgettable evidence—for him and for the nation—of their humility and dependency upon God. It is Jacob's greatest asset. And so it will be ours.

For me, this discovery was a wonderfully affirming word from God that He welcomed me to engage with Him—not in a mental discussion concerning my identity but in very real, personal, and sweaty soul-wrestling. God really does invite you and me into the ring, but it's a matter of intimacy rather than hostility! Enter if you dare. But you dare not refuse.

SOULSPACE PRESCRIPTION

This weekend, take a two-hour block of time and go somewhere nearby—a favorite place where you can be alone: a park, a creek, your church sanctuary, someplace quiet. Think about what issue(s) you and God are wrestling over. Ask Him what He is trying to tell you about your identity and your calling. (Hint: Sometimes it takes some digging to even figure out where the wrestling is in your life; don't give up!)

Fix Me,
I'm Broken

What you're after is truth from the inside out. Enter me, then,
conceive a new, true life. . . . God, make a fresh start in me, shape
a Genesis week from the chaos of my life.

—KING DAVID
PSALM 51:6 MSG

OUR COLORADO FALL was fast becoming a Colorado winter
when my heavenly Father gently drew me again into His
examining room. Our frequent snowfalls were a source of much joy
and wonder to us southerners. The kids would scramble to don layer
upon layer of clothing and then plead unrelentingly with us "old
folks" to accompany them out into the cold.

One of the wonderful things about snow is that its glossy white
smoothness covers over the rough, ugly brownness of the winter
ground. Our activities, in similar fashion, often conceal the ugly
woundedness of our souls, masking it with a veneer of great got-it-
togetherness. But once I'd stumbled into God's "medical" office, I
found Him gently softening and removing the scabs concealing my
hurts so He could bring His healing touch into my places of pain.

One of the wounds that had marked me in a very subconscious
way was an early label I had picked up as a child of being "lazy."

While not dwelt upon, this designation had appeared at key junctures in my life and had been absorbed into my identity. So, looking back over ten years of ministry, I found much of my soul clutter had been compounded by an underlying urgency to be busy. This cause-and-effect scenario is an example of the interplay between soul sickness and soul clutter. The pressures without—to be consumed with never-ending pastoral tasks—were affirmed by the pressures within to overcome my "laziness" and produce.

But . . . it was a lie.

SHEDDING THE LABELS

The remarkable revelation that appeared this October day—and was confirmed by the candor of my wife—was that I, Jerome Daley, am *not* a lazy person. No, I am not a driven, hyper workaholic, but neither am I lazy. Within my newfound soulspace, this truth suddenly flashed upon my consciousness.

I cannot express the relief and release I felt in making this simple discovery. Suddenly the pressure was off, and I didn't have anything left to prove. No one to impress with can-do, on-top-of-it pastoral skills. Fear is a powerful motivating force in life. But on this particular day this particular fear was broken. Ahhhhhh . . . it feels so good!

What are *your* labels? What boxes have been placed around you? If you don't know, it's good to ask yourself and ask God. The questions remind me of my favorite Max Lucado children's book, *You Are Special.* In it, a village of little wooden people called Wemmicks have been carefully fashioned by the Woodworker who lives in the workshop on the hill. Day by day, the Wemmicks go about their business, but as they do, they carry stickers they avidly place upon one another. When they like someone, they stick him or her with a gold star; if someone displeases them, he or she gets a gray dot.

So the Wemmicks go through their small lives acquiring a collection of other Wemmicks' declarations concerning their value. The allegory is simply and profoundly accurate . . . and deeply disturbing. As the story develops, it becomes known that those who hang out with the Woodworker up on the hill become sticker-free: When someone tries to place either a dot or a star upon them, it simply falls to the ground. What a glorious thought—that we could be equally free of other people's determinations upon our lives, both the good and the bad!

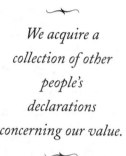

We acquire a collection of other people's declarations concerning our value.

I can't think of a better picture for the soul-healing our Creator and Sustainer offers us.

APPROACHING GOD FOR REPAIRS

Psalm 127:1 says that "unless the LORD builds the house, its builders labor in vain." So when it comes to reconditioning our lives for soul health, it has to be a God thing! Only the Lord can repair us and re-create us toward the image for which we are destined. The construction of your soul will look different than mine, but both will be things of marvel and beauty—if, and only if, God is the architect.

The reconstruction of our lives varies according to our unique blueprints, but it is not uncommon for most of us to experience a layering effect that involves bouncing back and forth between re-calibrating our original design and restoring the damage of misuse. Personally, I found my soul on alternating worktables as God renewed my future (my identity and calling) and repaired my past (my brokenness and woundedness). As He moved me from one table to the other, each step inevitably took me deeper toward the real issues; it was as though God were peeling me like an onion. This is not always a pleasant experience, but it is so very important. It's what my friend Russ calls "scary good"!

My goal in this chapter is not to attempt to broad-brush inner healing, nor even to focus upon one or two facets of this worthy subject. Instead, I want to impart the conviction that allowing God to process and heal your soul sickness is essential to soul health. Second, I want to impress you with the fact that healing the soul is very difficult, if not downright impossible, without a lifestyle of soulspace. Third, I want to share some of my personal experiences with healing to encourage and inspire you toward that goal.

Removing the Scab, Healing the Wound

An unhealed past has the terrible power to ball-and-chain us to old, destructive forces and successfully shut down our true destinies. Back in chapter 3, I began to differentiate between soul clutter and soul sickness: Clutter attacks our *doing* while sickness infects our *being*. Clutter is generated more by our activities and affects our rela-tionships; sickness is usually generated by our relationships and affects our activities. Viewing my life through these lenses, I began to see quick and dramatic changes in terms of removing clutter; however, the healing of my soul sickness required a much deeper and somewhat longer process.

Other people's determinations had marked me; I had to admit that truth. I had picked up a lot of "stickers" from people, as most of us have, particularly from my classmates at school. As a result, I had to further admit that my fear of people's opinions had been a defining influence upon my life and my life roles—as a pastor, as a husband, as a person. I had shaped and molded my actions and my personality to make other people happy and to avoid criticism. So I would be liked. So I would be okay.

Soul clutter attacks our doing while soul sickness infects our being!

Let me get more specific. Before Kellie and I made the leap from North Carolina to Colorado, we met with another pastor and his wife for some counsel. During that time together, this pastor gained some discernment about me, sensing that something had happened in my life when I was five years old that still affected me in important ways. I didn't know what to do with his comment at the time, so I just told him we would pray about it. Occasionally over the next weeks, I prayed and thought about it but never got any insight. I even asked my mother if she knew of any important event that had occurred when I was five. Nothing.

Months later, I mentioned it in passing to our dear friend and faithful intercessor, Susy. She later e-mailed me some impressions she had received in prayer. She told me at that young age I had been publicly "called on the carpet" for something, and that shame and embarrassment had entered my soul. I then resolved, she saw, never to be put in that position again. That self-protecting vow had opened the door for an ongoing fear of others and their opinions of me.

When I read that e-mail, I immediately remembered a scene from first grade. Now, you have to understand that I have a notoriously bad memory in general, but this moment in time from thirty years ago is vividly etched in my mind. I was friends with a girl named Karla; our families were close, and we often played together. Well, on the playground one day at recess, she thought in little-girl fashion that it would be fun for us to hold hands. Liking Karla and being astonishingly naïve, I agreed. So there we were, two little first-graders holding hands out on the playground, when we caught the attention of a group of boys who began taunting us with the ubiquitous sing-song chant, "Jerome and Karla sitting in a tree, k-i-s-s-i-n-g. First comes loves, then comes marriage, then comes Jerome with a baby carriage." I was mortified, or in Susy's words, "shamed and embarrassed"—so much so that I abandoned Karla and ran away across the playground to safety.

I am sure similar scenes have taken place in the lives of many, many other young boys and girls. On the one hand, these incidents educate us to the way people, and children in particular, can find pleasure in the discomfort of others. On the other hand, I can see how, for myself, this seemingly innocuous event marked my impressionable soul and reinforced my natural fear of others' opinions in such a way that I still live under its effects.

Seeing the problem, as the proverb goes, is truly half the battle. So when you and I get these kinds of illuminations in prayer or from other trustworthy people, we need to recognize them as God's avenues for bringing the healing our souls so desperately need. The power of God removes the scabs from these soul injuries and exposes every form of shame and pain from past hurts. Then He retrains our souls to believe the wonderful truth that comes from His mouth. That process is life-changing! It is soul-transforming.

God can work this transformation in many different ways, but the result is the same: Through His enlightenment we come to understand how our souls have been sick from the ongoing effects of old wounds, then we let the hand of God come with its healing touch.

Simply consider the place healing occupied in the earthly ministry of Jesus. More than any other recorded action, we see Jesus bringing the Kingdom rule of heaven to earth by removing the effects of physical and emotional trauma. And His plan has not changed one whit today.

At the most basic level, our souls are sick because of sin, because we are deceived about what is right and what is wrong. I am convinced that our actions betray what we truly believe; we do the things that our hearts honestly think will bring us joy or minimize our pain. But of course we are frequently wrong! When we don't trust the accuracy of God's wisdom, we act

Our actions betray what we truly believe.

like the kid in a candy shop who disregards the proprietor's warnings and eats himself sick. We all share in sin through our humanity, but Romans 6 describes how God's grace evicts the tyranny of sin and brings God's children within the redeeming rule of heaven. When we oppose that redemption and opt out of that freedom clause, we remain slaves to our deceptions.

Sin remains an issue within our souls, even as sons and daughters of the Kingdom, as long as we inhabit planet earth. We relate painfully well to the pathos Paul expressed in Romans 7:18–19: "For I have the desire to do what is good, but I cannot carry it out. For what I do is not the good I want to do; no, the evil I do not want to do—this I keep on doing." Our sins and the sins of others continue to impact our lives. Their influence takes place on the level of the soul: Instead of our minds, emotions, and wills being shaped by the Holy Spirit through an open, uncluttered window to our spirits, we find the window boarded up and an old, familiar enemy directing the drama of our thoughts, feelings, and desires!

When God first rescued us, our spirits were transformed and revived, as I described earlier. Our spirits were entirely infused with the quality of heaven and became the residing place for the Holy Spirit, or the "temple of the Holy Spirit," as 1 Corinthians 6:19 says. There is no sin or death residing in our "spirit-temple" any longer. Our souls, on the other hand, remain infected with the virus of sin, revealing a strong self-orientation and susceptibility to deception. This sin-identity is no longer our true self as it once was (see Romans 6:17), but it operates as an impostor within us as long as we remain on planet earth, and its operation reinforces sickness of the soul.

Diagnosing Our Disease

Soul sickness is like having bark beetles invade our tree. Remember the two crucial trees in the Garden of Eden, the tree of life and the tree of the knowledge of good and evil? The latter I described earlier as the tree that grows out of the world system. Well, if the tree of the knowledge of good and evil represents our own sinful tendencies, then the gnawing work of those soul-sickness "beetles" makes us greatly susceptible to injury from other people. Hurtful words, personal rejection, the tearing down of hopes and aspirations, and the marring of the inner image of God within us—we are all familiar with such damage. And we all bear the marks of it, not on our skin usually but upon our hearts.

Okay. It's time to ask the infamous "So what?" question: *So what if we've been wounded in the past? That's life,* you may say. *We've got to get over it and move on!*

Yes, getting past our past and moving forward is exactly our goal. But it's easier said than done. Despite our desire to get beyond the effects of past hurts, most of us still carry around untreated, and frequently unrealized, soul sickness. And until that sickness is diagnosed and healed by the Spirit of God, we cannot truly be free. Like the bark beetles, these wounds cause deep and covert destruction within our souls.

What kind of destruction? Well, this enemy attacks the very identities we were seeking to uncover in the last chapter. The search for our true selves is hampered greatly by undiagnosed soul sickness because we may live underneath the weight of lies communicated to us, accepting as truth such hellish statements as, "You're just stupid!" or "You will never get it right!" Or, conversely, we will live in reaction to people's judgments, trying to compensate for perceived weaknesses by fashioning what Brent Curtis and John Eldredge call our "false selves." Feeling ourselves to be deficient in some realm, usually because of a wound we carry, we wrap ourselves around a perceived strength and so develop a caricature of our intended nature, a false self that appears strong. And then we hide behind that false self while the wound goes untreated.

The damage caused by beetles of soul sickness appears as

> *Anger at others, anger at circumstances, anger at yourself—these are clues that woundedness is untreated within your soul.*

damaged leaves on our trees, and the symptoms are not pretty: *anger, confusion,* and *apathy,* to name a few. The very anger I encountered in my journey toward freedom was a red flag of warning: Beneath the "bark" of my life, bad things were at work! Anger at others, anger at circumstances, anger at yourself—these are clues that woundedness is untreated within your soul.

Or woundedness may express itself as confusion: inability to keep a job, frequent career changes, mate changes, or energy that is shotgunned in dozens of different directions without a clear, overriding vision. In others, woundedness short-circuits the will so that apathy pervades the wounded ones' existence; they withdraw from all challenges and risks, too tired or afraid to dig into their missing identities.

But it need not be this way! The treatment for healing our woundedness, thank God, is simple. Not easy, but simple: *Recognition. Forgiveness. Release.*

God's power is overwhelmingly able to dispatch the effects of soul sickness and heal their scars, but the wound unheeded is the wound untreated. Many who dismiss the pursuit of inner healing as a weak, self-absorbed, and unproductive enterprise attempt to simply write off the past, but they cannot seem to move beyond its defining mark on their own lives. At the core of every wound is a lie—a fundamental untruth believed about ourselves, about God, or about other people.[1] It is the job of the Holy Spirit, our Comforter and Counselor, to unearth that lie and speak His healing truth into it as a salve for the soul.

LIVING IN THE TREE OF LIFE

When we begin to grapple with our woundedness, it leads us eventually to its opposite: wholeness. We spent some time back in chapter 3 looking at the tree of the knowledge of good and evil—the structure that typifies the world system—and in this chapter we've discussed how that system infects our souls. So now maybe you're thinking, *I know what soul damage looks like, but what does wholeness look like?* To answer that question, let's turn now to the tree of life to understand how God intends to build our lives as deposits of heaven on earth. This tree also has roots, branches, and fruit, and it mirrors the life we long for. The life we were made for!

Healing is simple.
Not easy, but simple:
Recognition.
Forgiveness.
Release.

In contrast to the roots of fear, greed, and pride, God's Kingdom is rooted in *love, faith,* and *humility.* Of all virtues, these three appear to be most foundational in the life to which God calls us.

In Romans 13:10, Paul declared unabashedly that *love* is the fulfillment of the entire law of God. And God captures His own essence in a word, defining Himself as "love" in 1 John 4:8, 16.

Faith, Paul declared in Romans 14:23, is so fundamental to the life of God that whatever is not done in faith is, in fact, sin. When the writer of Hebrews set up the "hall of fame," as it were, for famous men and women of God throughout biblical history, the defining qualification was their faith.

Finally, *humility* lies at the core of Jesus—both His teaching and His example. The greatest sermon we have from Jesus is what we call the Sermon on the Mount, reported in Matthew 5–7; in that sermon the theme pervading His description of the Kingdom is humility. Just look at the Beatitudes through those lenses! And Philippians 2 points to the defining quality of humility in Jesus' life. The list goes on and on.

**The Tree
of Life**

LOVE   HUMILITY

FAITH

So what does that mean for us? What does it mean for our lives to be rooted in love, faith, and humility? The question cannot be answered in any meaningful way in a simple paragraph. We answer it most honestly and truly by the testimony of our lives. But we can ask ourselves some questions that will bear upon our pursuit of that kind of life:

1. What parts of my home life and work life are lived for the good of others, and what parts are lived to satisfy my own desires?

2. To an outside observer, what specific actions in my life would demonstrate a fundamental reliance upon God rather than myself?

3. Would those who know me best describe me as approachable, teachable, easy to work with, easy to correct, and not easily offended?

If you're still not sure whether your life is rooted in love, faith, and humility, then let's look at the branches of the tree of life and see if they reveal the motivations of your heart: *service, trust,* and *worship.*

The life rooted in love for God and others (remember the two greatest commandments?) will branch into *service* for both God and people. When you love people you invest your time, money, and energy in relationships . . . more than in programs and activities.

The practical outgrowth of faith is a steadfast *trust,* or *confidence,* in the goodness and power of God (see Psalm 62:11), which produces a deep-seated security that weathers the inevitable storms of life.

Next, the heart of humility readily expresses itself in *worship,* realizing intuitively that we are created for our heavenly Father's pleasure and purpose and are utterly dependent upon Him.

Still not sure what tree you're living in? Well, the root, as they

**Tree of Life
Outgrowths**

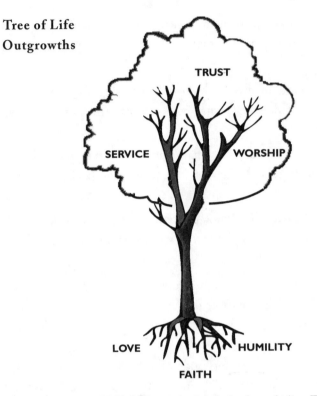

say, is in the fruit. In other words, fruit doesn't lie. Fruit always shows the character that's there, or isn't there. Character is what's left when the mortar of relationships and the pestle of circumstances grind you up.

Romans 14:17 says that the Kingdom of God will be demonstrated in three specific qualities: Righteousness. Peace. Joy. And it's no mystery why this is so. A life of worship, a consistently Godward life, will certainly express itself in actions and attitudes that God likes. Thus there is *righteousness*. And a trusting heart is a *peaceful* heart, because an abiding security is the antithesis of anxiety.

Finally, a life characterized by service to others will never cease to be a life of *joy*. It's amazing how smart God is!

Root Virtues	Heart-Motivations	Soul Health
Love ⟶	Service ⟶	Joy
Faith ⟶	Trust ⟶	Peace
Humility ⟶	Worship ⟶	Righteousness

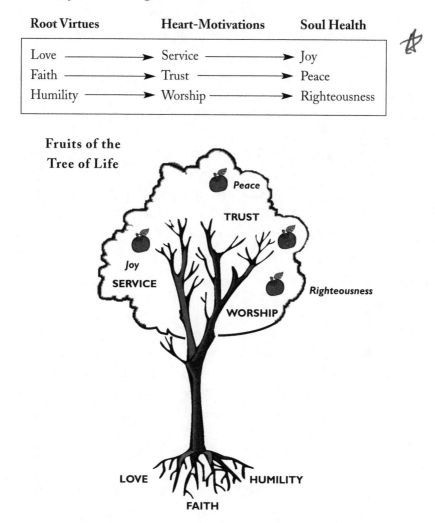

Fruits of the Tree of Life

The healing of your soul comes from living in the tree of life. As the apostle John wrote, "On each side of the river stood the tree of life. . . . And the leaves of the tree are for the healing of the nations" (Revelation 22:2). The choice of where and how we'll live awaits us a hundred times a day in a hundred little choices: Life or death. Blessing or cursing. Truth or lie. Pick your tree.

My greatest hope in writing this chapter is not that you will remember my story but that you will come away with the conviction that inner healing can only realistically occur in an environment of soulspace. That you will be motivated and encouraged by one more reason to carve out space in your lifestyle: the fact that a cluttered soul will never even find its wounds, much less pursue the path of healing! Please believe me on this. Your soul will never experience lasting health without adequate time to reflect and respond, without space to ponder and pray.

Living Waters

The final picture I'd like to offer of God's redeeming, transforming work to heal our souls comes from C. S. Lewis's inspired fiction series, *The Chronicles of Narnia*. My personal favorite of the chronicles is *The Voyage of the Dawn Treader*, in which a foul-hearted boy named Eustace is accidentally turned into a dragon as a result of his own greed. Through this scaly experience, Eustace comes to see himself as others see him . . . and realizes what a beast he has been to the others.

In a dreamlike nightly visitation, the great lion, Aslan, leads Eustace the dragon up a mountain to a garden pool whose refreshing coolness makes Eustace long to bathe in it. But before

Eustace can enter, Aslan tells him that if he would like to bathe, he must first undress, that he cannot bathe as he is. Since, as a dragon, Eustace is not wearing any clothes, he is unsure how to begin. He starts to tear at his painful, scaly hide with his long claws. To his surprise, he begins to shed his entire skin and finally steps out of it completely. But, stepping down into the water, he is dismayed to see in his reflection that the same ugly hide is still upon him.

Again he tears through his scaly skin and steps out of it, only to find another layer . . . and another. Finally Aslan speaks up and says that *he*, Aslan, must do the undressing! Eustace describes the experience this way:

> The very first tear was so deep, I thought it had gone right into my heart. And when he began pulling the skin off, it hurt worse than anything I've ever felt. The only thing that made me able to bear it was just the pleasure of feeling the stuff peel off. . . . Then he caught hold of me . . . and threw me into the water. It smarted like anything, but only for a moment. After that it became perfectly delicious and as soon as I started swimming and splashing I found that all the pain had gone.[2]

I love this illustration of God's wonderful work in our lives. We cannot heal ourselves; that much we know. *Most* of us know it, anyway. But when we submit ourselves completely to the mercy of our Maker, we experience the deepest and truest renewal of heart—a renewal we may have given up as lost altogether. This "undragoning" process is painful, but it is the way, *the only way*, to lasting refreshment. The healing of our soul sickness occurs one layer at a time.

SOULSPACE PRESCRIPTION

Right this moment, take several minutes to ponder what layer of soul sickness God is stripping off of you—or wanting to strip away. Invite Him into that place of pain and hear what He has to say to you. If you hear nothing, then the layers are hidden (or perhaps healed), but if you sense that something is there, make it a matter of daily prayer throughout the coming week. Make no mistake: God is in the business of "undragoning" us!

chapter seven

Cleaning House

Accepting no substitutes for what we really want leads to simplicity of life.

—BRENNAN MANNING

LATE ONE AFTERNOON before the "diner epiphany," I was walking down the back stairwell in our North Carolina home when I paused for a second, disgusted to notice the two-inch strip of electric blue paint that lined the doorjamb—the remnants of an unfinished project from nearly two years earlier when we had moved in and painted the surrounding wall a more acceptable taupe. Still standing there, my mind flitted uncomfortably to the swing-set anchors lying in their dusty box in the garage—instead of where they ought to be: driven into the ground in the backyard to secure the poles of the swing set.

Suddenly an unsummoned tidal wave of frustrations swept over me: the hedges growing out of control along the front of the house, the dead azaleas in the front flower bed needing replacement, the half-finished circle of pavers in the patio-to-be out back, the bank statements unbalanced for several months in a row, the teetering towers of paperwork threatening to avalanche my home office. The homeowners association meeting was set for later that evening, and I knew I really ought to go and cultivate neighborhood relationships. Two kids were fighting in the background while the other complained about what was for dinner. Kellie was frazzled by a hectic day of homeschooling, homecleaning, and homecooking, not to mention planning the upcoming ladies ministry retreat.

Is this my castle, I wondered? *My peaceful haven, my sanctuary from the stormy world out there? I really ought to go spend some time with the kids. Ought to help Kellie out with dinner. Ought to tackle the lawn in the last hour of daylight. But . . . heck, I've had a demanding day! When do I get some time for me? I deserve a little time to unwind, right?* I brushed the Tinkertoys off my recliner and picked up the newspaper.

Inspiring, isn't it!

"There's no place like home," Dorothy said, and how right she was. There is nowhere else as potentially satisfying and securing as home—and nowhere else as potentially denigrating and devastating. The home holds our greatest challenges and our truest rewards. But like the other components of our lives, our homes have been invaded by the persistent programming of our have-it-all, do-it-all world-system culture. Space seems a distant memory—a peaceful image hidden back in our pre-kids, early married days or maybe all the way back in our years as singles.

Once upon a time, we were able to do what we wanted . . . without so many responsibilities and expectations pressing down on us, crushing the life out of us. Well . . . maybe. Or maybe not. We frequently project our current yearnings back upon a golden age in which our memories conveniently filter out the stresses of that prior life. But the image remains—a haunting ache for a simpler world.

In our most honest moments, we know we were made for lives more peaceful, more joyful, more free. Yet, caught up in our addictions, we continue to choose clutter and chaos. It's a way of life, and we don't know how to live otherwise.

THE INITIAL CONTRADICTION

Ironically, discovering God as our Father and embracing the forgiveness and calling of a spiritual life tends to make matters worse, not better. Because now there is a war in earnest—a contest between the outpost of heaven occupying our spirits and the systematic habits of the world embedded in our souls. Our schizophrenia defies the

Lasting change happens from the inside out.

canned offerings of the well-meaning as well as the religious calisthenics of the performers. And the pain grows.

This contradiction occurs by design. Pain has power like few other things to illuminate hidden disease, whether in the body or the soul, and to motivate us toward treatment and healing. Pain in our homes will eventually show the character of our homes—whether we will run to escape the pain or we will bring our attention and effort to bear upon the needed solutions.

CREATING EMOTIONAL SPACE

Where do the solutions begin for redeeming the climates in our homes? How do we bring the restorative power of heaven to bear on our family dynamics? The foundational girder underlying all the principles discussed in this book is that *lasting change happens from the inside out.* No supply of directions and disciplines can effect lasting changes in the character of our homes. It begins in the heart!

What exactly begins in the heart? *Conviction*—the recognition that worldly and selfish motivations have robbed our homes and our souls of our spiritual destiny. *Repentance*—the determination to change direction and to pursue the life of the Kingdom. *Humility*—the willingness to seek out new paradigms and new patterns for home priorities. *Perseverance*—the commitment to press toward freedom in the face of disappointments and failures. *Passion*—the desire for intimacy with God that fuels our pursuit of His presence as the central focus of our homes.

> *The greatest enemy to space in the home is dissipation.*

The greatest enemy to space in the home is *dissipation.* Brennan Manning wrote, "When we are dissipated through busyness, obsession, addiction, mindlessness, and preoccupation with television, sports, gossip, movies, shallow reading, and so forth, we cannot be attentive to the gifts that arrive each day."[1] Most of the things that we as Christians fill our lives and homes with are not bad things. Television, for example, is not an inherently bad thing, but I don't know of any one activity that dissipates soulspace more effectively in our lives! Manning contends that these dissipating forces keep us from paying attention to what really matters. They keep us trapped in trivia while the spiritual heritage of our families is plundered. We must awaken ourselves from this anesthetized stupor and recover our homes. The Kingdom of God hinges upon the home!

Battling Emotional Space-Stealers

Space is very, very practical. In this chapter I am drawing from personal discoveries and principles we have discussed throughout the book and applying them to many of the practical challenges of crafting an environment of space right where we live.

Absolutely essential to a healthy home is *emotional space.* In fact, I would go so far as to say that it is the defining issue in the spiritual health of a marriage and children. Emotional space is what allows us to emerge from the cocoons of our work, our school, our occupations, and our other small worlds and invest ourselves in other people. We cannot understand or connect meaningfully with the people we love most if, to use a computer analogy, all our "RAM" is maxed out on maintaining ourselves!

Television. So, to continue the computer analogy, what robs our system resources and so depletes our emotional space? I have already landed a blow upon television, so let me share our story on this one. I was not a TV addict. I probably watched it two to three nights a week for an hour or two. However, whenever I did watch, I went comatose! I did not hear or see any other living thing until the program was over. If a kid was screaming, I just turned up the volume. I was a brain-dead lump of carbon until the TV was turned off. I score this thing

> family relationships: 0
>
> entertainment: marginal
>
> soulspace: in the red

Let's face it: The entire vitality and atmosphere of a family may rest upon how you use the couple of hours between dinner and bed. You can invest it or waste it.

Once again, Kellie was the perceptive one in our family. For several years she hinted that we ought to just get rid of the one-eyed beast. But I wasn't ready. I suppose the pain wasn't high enough yet to move me. But I can tell you that leaving our TV behind when we moved to Colorado offered our family an immense contribution toward emotional space.

Unnecessary Information. What else robs our attention and burns up precious minutes and hours? Unnecessary information is a biggie. The cumulative effect of newspapers, Internet, magazines, video games, catalogs, radio, and telephone can positively crush all unassigned space in a home. When you recognize that the point of space is to have "free" time to spend on meaningful interactions with one another and with God, you realize how destructive this overload of news and messages can be. Every mode of media has a valid function (with the arguable exception of video games), but we must become attentive enough to gauge its impact, individually and cumulatively, upon the health of the home.

Extracurricular Activities. Another threat is extracurricular activities. They can absolutely consume school-age children—and their parents! It is wonderful to have so many options available to kids these days—every conceivable sport, hobby, community group, church group, music lesson, and school club imaginable. But multiply the number of activities times the number of children you have times the number of car trips you have to make, and *poof!* Space is a distant memory. There is a good reason why Henry Cloud and John Townsend's insightful book *Boundaries* has sold so prolifically— because we don't have them! Yet we desperately need them. Our families' emotional space depends upon our willingness to set boundaries to protect what is important in our homes.

If our children are to gain any grasp on this kind of space for their lives, guess where it has to come from! They aren't going to find it at school, they aren't going to find it at the mall (talk about soul clutter!), and they may not find much at church. So, like most things, it falls to us parents to impart these values in tangible ways.

The Tendency to Want More. Next, consider the realm of advertising and shopping in the context of space-stealers. Of course, occasional shopping is necessary and can sometimes be relaxing and entertaining, but we mustn't be naïve. The entire design of advertising is to manufacture discontent and feed our innate tendency to want more. The entire goal of retailers is to overwhelm our senses with their razzle-dazzle and lull us into what may be irrational, unwise, or unnecessary purchases. Not only are many of us addicted to shopping, but it can consume space in a great many venues—emotional space, time space, and financial space, for starters. In the quest to regain this lost space, we have to learn to see beyond appearances—beyond the way everyone else does it—and to recognize the impact of each action upon our quality of inner life.

Space depends upon your willingness to set boundaries to protect what is important.

The subject of financial space bears special mention. The cultural standard is now to spend more than we earn; we all feel the tug upon our souls for instant gratification. Unsecured debt is skyrocketing in its current acceptance as normal behavior—much to the destruction of emotional space. One has only to count the daily barrage of junk mail (and now junk e-mail!) offering credit cards and debt-consolidation packages. A commitment to space seeks to simplify life, reduce debt with its concomitant burden and stress, and limit the accumulation of material stuff. By definition, space means setting aside financial resources to build a buffer, a reserve, a margin so as to multiply freedom in our home life.

Other Space-Stealers. We have many susceptibilities to emotional clutter. The Internet can gobble up hundreds of priceless hours with very little to show for it. Sports addictions are expected, appreciated, and socially rewarded, but the payback is felt in lack of family intimacy, soul health, and spiritual vitality. The workshop, the garage, the hobby—anything can displace the priority of family relationships. To this dilemma, Romans 12:2 speaks forcefully:

> Don't become so well-adjusted to your culture that you fit into it without even thinking. Instead, fix your attention on God. You'll be changed from the inside out. (MSG)

Since moving to Colorado and making radical choices for space (they're not that radical really; they just appear so in relation to cultural expectations), our family dynamics have improved steadily and wonderfully. I can remember, two years ago, crying out to the Lord for an atmosphere of love and peace in our home but feeling impotent to change it. Today, I still see room for improvement, but I also revel in substantial transformations from confusion toward harmony and from contention toward teamwork. Beyond emotional space, several of these results are due to changes in some key relational tools we have learned.

NURTURING SPACE SKILLS AND STRENGTHS

As a climate of space is established in your home, you can begin to mold the shape and strength of your family. In our experience, three skills have made a lasting impact upon our relationships: demonstrated love, customized communication, and respectful discipline. And while this discussion is directed at those with families, the dynamics also apply to those who are unmarried and have no children. Love languages, communication styles, and control issues are vital to your primary relationships—close friends, co-workers, parents, etc. The earlier and better you learn these skills, the healthier your relationships will be throughout your lifetime.

Demonstrated Love

The components of demonstrated love come directly from Gary Chapman's tremendous book *The Love Languages*. In entertaining fashion, Chapman highlights five dominant ways—"languages," in his terminology—in which people give and receive love.

Without stealing Chapman's thunder, I'll wet your appetite by borrowing an example. It would not be uncommon for a husband and wife to speak different love languages; for instance, the guy may communicate his love through physical touch while his wife may communicate her love through acts of service—cooking meals, cleaning the house, whatever. The point of the book is that we must understand what is received as love by each member of the family in order to learn that person's "language." By doing so we demonstrate the love we have in ways that deeply impact the hearts of our spouse and children! Within the context of home space, this skill alone will generate tremendous dividends.

Customized Communication

Some of us communicate best by talking; some interact best visually, either by physical demonstration or through word pictures; others are extremely tactile and have to actually *do* something in order to understand what is being communicated. This concept of customized communication carries tremendous ramifications within family relationships. One child can be easily directed with a simple instruction while another child requires a written list in order to succeed. A third child needs you to take his or her little face in your hands, get nose-to-nose, and explain a project, whether it's homework or cleaning up the bedroom. You may even have to go with that one and show him or her exactly what you are expecting.

Understanding your spouse works the same way and positions your relationship to prosper or, alternately, to be in continuing conflict. For example, Kellie has come to understand (though not appreciate) my severe forgetfulness. After many moons of butting heads and having hurt feelings on both sides, we discovered the amazing new technology of writing notes for me. We've learned that if it needs to be remembered by me, it needs to be written down. So she writes notes. I write notes. Yes, I am very visual . . . and brain-damaged! After several years of therapy, I'm fine now. Really, I am.

Respectful Discipline

In the family environment, there is perhaps no issue as troublesome as that of providing effective correction and discipline for children. Of the reams of instruction that have been or could be offered, I want to focus on one pivotal dynamic that has helped our home in wonderful ways: *respect.*

As parents of an eight-year-old, a six-year-old, and a four-year-old, Kellie and I wield great power over our children both emotionally and physically, and that is a fearsome responsibility. Within the biblical mandate to instruct and correct, our humanness is woefully susceptible to misusing our authority in destructive ways. It is crucial to differentiate control and management in our parenting styles. The difference between control and management, in any application of leadership, is a recognition of and respect for the will of another. To dominate or crush the will of another, even of a child, is to injure the image of God within that one. Breaking the will of a child, though popular Christian terminology, is not biblical terminology.

The biblical instruction itself is somewhat vague at this point, relying upon broader character instruction for men and women to form the basis for parenting with intelligence and integrity. The familiar call to obedience for children in Ephesians 6:1–3 is amplified in 1 Timothy 3:4, where Paul included in his qualifications for an elder the charge to "manage his own family well and see that his children obey him with proper respect." The goal of biblical parenting is clearly that children receive instruction, come to own the standards of their parents, and live out a heartfelt obedience. But how to pull off this accomplishment is the challenging part.

It is crucial to differentiate between control and management.

Does respecting the will of our children mean letting them have their own way? Not at all. The way God has led Kellie and me is to set firm boundaries on the essentials of safety and family function: *No, you may not play in the street. Yes, you do have a bedtime.* Bear in mind that good parenting equips children with the ability to control themselves, giving them the tools to govern their own wills more and more as they grow.

An incredibly powerful way to do this is by giving them age-appropriate choices: *If you try your peas, you may have dessert; if you throw your peas at your sister, you will skip dessert.* Grappling with life choices and dealing with the consequences of right and wrong decisions empowers children to learn the self-control that will serve them far better in life than mindless submission to the enforced dictates of Mom and Dad. Much more could be said here, but my purpose is simply to share the seed of a life-giving revelation we have experienced in our home.

CREATING SPIRITUAL SPACE

Bzzz . . . Bzzz . . . Bzzz . . . The rhythmic pulse of my alarm clock jarred me into semiconsciousness well before it was light outside. An early bird I am not! Though almost all of my thirty-six years have been tied to early-rising routines, it is still difficult for me to force my feet out of that warm bed and onto the floor. Some of my most miserable memories are from a five-month stint with the United Parcel Service, when I had to rise at three o'clock every morning for the rewarding task of pulling thousands of boxes out of semi-trucks and pushing them onto uphill rollers (where they promptly tried to slide back into the truck) and then onto conveyor belts . . . all the while listening to the supervisor yell at us! (Do you wonder why I needed emotional healing?)

In Colorado, however, I found that one of the rewards of going TV-less was the ease of going to bed early. Now, after getting the kids bedded down, Kellie and I usually spend an hour or so reconnecting from the day before we head to bed ourselves.

Despite my daily contention with the alarm clock, I have intentionally chosen an early lifestyle in order to invest the very first part of my day with the One I love most. There is simply no substitute for making space for the spiritual at the beginning of the day!

Despite the importance I place on creating *spiritual* space, I purposefully began this chapter with a discussion about *emotional* space because, strangely, emotional space precedes the spiritual. Not in theory but in practice. If you do not retrain your soul in the priority of space, actively creating room in your thinking, feeling, and willing, then your spiritual efforts default into obligations, mere qualifications for your spiritual performance. Funny how that works.

> *There is simply no substitute for making spiritual space at the beginning of the day!*

The same cultivation of emotional space that enlarges our family intimacy transfers largely to our spiritual space—our relationship with God. When our lives cease to be driven by production, then we become capable of simply being with God and allowing our time to unfold with Him in a supernaturally natural way . . . without the old pressures of having to do this or accomplish that in order for these times to "count."

Now let me offer some practical ways to carve out spiritual space in your home.

Pray Together

Probably the single most powerful thing you can do to create spiritual space if you are married is to pray daily with your spouse. Not as a replacement for your own one-on-one time with God, but together with your husband or wife. Spouse-prayer is like doing aerobics with weights: You are multiplying your efforts on several fronts simultaneously.

Prayer with your wife or husband strengthens your own prayer life with God by expanding your prayer vocabulary, prayer style, and prayer targets. Next, it multiplies your power in prayer, per Deuteronomy 32:30 ("How could one man chase a thousand, or two put ten thousand to flight . . . ?"). In addition, it brings the two of you into greater agreement regarding everything—your children, your work, your day, your future, your ministry.

I find that these times of prayer between Kellie and myself often birth important spiritual discussions in which we come to understand one another better and discern the mind of the Lord in this atmosphere of His presence. Things are shared between us in this place that would never come up in times of casual conversation.

Cultivate Your Children's Spiritual Worlds

Spiritual space in your home is enlarged by making time to talk with your children about God, to pray with them about the issues of their little worlds, and to bring them into your spiritual journey. This can be done at many times and in various places—from table prayers to bedtime prayers to family times to spontaneous moments of opportunity. You don't need to implement a rigid regimen of indoctrination with your kids; just look for and capitalize on the daily lessons of life.

Rehearse the spiritual lessons of school and neighborhood as well as Sunday school. Worship together. Serve the poor together. Tithe and give offerings together. Remember and rehearse the landmark events of God's intervention in your family history.

Speak blessings over your children, affirming who they are in Christ and who they are becoming. It's not a matter of finding the perfect curriculum; it's a matter of taking ownership of your children's spiritual well-being!

Again I must emphasize that space doesn't come from merely imposing more activities on the family, even spiritual ones. Simplifying and streamlining your home comes from the inside: The more your heart is awakened to awareness of God and gratitude to Him for all His workings in your daily details, the more you will listen and look for Him, the more you will enjoy your communion with Him in the very midst of life, and the more you will convey this fundamental life-orientation to your children, your friends, and all within your sphere of influence!

CREATING PHYSICAL SPACE

My final topic in this chapter is the influence of your physical home upon your soul condition. The amount of space or clutter that characterizes your natural living environment is a pretty good gauge of your inner soul environment. A home that is consistently messy, disorganized, or dirty will fight against your efforts toward inner space.

I am not saying that everyone has to be Martha Stewart; I would never add those expectations to our existing performance pressures. Rather, I am making a call for integrity—that we approach all of life with the same motivations. We all have a slightly different threshold of discomfort with mess and clutter, but at some point we all feel conflicted and motivated to bring order to the clutter. Let your motivation for physical space set the tone for your desired soulspace. And vice versa.

Confession time. My biggest struggle with physical space is my desk. I have an exemplary vision for filing and organization and efficiency. Unfortunately, it ends with vision and doesn't extend to actual doing. It took my friend Bruce walking through my home one day and noting the ironic disconnect between my "talk" on space and my "walk" of desk chaos to enlighten me with this important connection. It's still hard for me, but I work toward that goal in order to enjoy its reward.

A messy home will fight against your efforts toward inner space.

I'd like to address one additional concern related to physical space, and that is avoiding the trap of *perfectionism*. Most of us struggle at times with the feelings that our value is related to our performance, and we're never satisfied with our performance. A much smaller percentage of the population is extraordinarily vested with performance skills and is able to come much closer to the mark. Frequently, these few will gladly wear the badge of "perfectionist" and incorporate this drivenness into their identity.

Please don't do that. To take on the identity of a perfectionist is to willfully cast yourself into a pit of torturous examination. As a perfectionist, you are forced to constantly evaluate your own performance (and the performance of others) with devastating results: Either you fail your own evaluation and succumb to consequential guilt and condemnation, or you pass your own evaluation and evolve into consequential pride and judgmentalism. It's a lose-lose proposition, and it puts you in direct conflict with the very grace of God your soul craves. Perfectionism is a disease of the tree of the knowledge of good and evil; its antidote lies in embracing the tree of life with its foundation of humility, faith, and love.

SOULSPACE PRESCRIPTION

Think of the person you know who has the most emotional space and soul health in his or her life. Make an appointment to sit down with that person and discuss what has worked for him or her, then consider where you would like to see changes in your own lifestyle.

chapter eight

Into the Scary World
of Intimacy

I hope you never fear those mountains in the distance, never
settle for the path of least resistance. Living might mean taking
chances, but they're worth taking; loving might be a mistake, but
it's worth making.... And when you get the chance to sit it out or
dance, I hope you dance!

—"I Hope You Dance"
MARK SANDERS AND TIA SILLERS

INTIMACY IS EVERYTHING. Intimacy with God. Intimacy with
people. In September 2000, Kellie and I began preparing for the
annual Wilder Weekend, a family tradition that, for the first time in
its ten-year history, would be held outside of North Carolina at our
place in the beautiful Colorado mountains. On the first weekend of
each November, all of Kellie's siblings—the Wilder kids—and their
spouses converge on one location to spend three packed days
together. Ditching our kids in appropriate places, the ten of us
come together to play, eat, tell stories, eat, pray together, eat some
more—basically to enlarge our lives with one another!

This tradition began the first year we were married and has continued through our years to become something we look forward to
with great expectation. So those months of September and October
2000 were filled with dreaming and scheming of how we could make
this weekend a delightful time of togetherness, worthy of the travel

it would require of Kellie's siblings who lived in the East. In years past we had discovered that the soul-sharing and friendship-building in those three intentional days eclipsed the other 362 by far!

Finally the big weekend came, and after playing merry-go-round in the Denver airport, we rounded up our herd and carted them back to Manitou Springs for refreshments, tantalizing them with plans for horseback rides through the surreal Garden of the Gods and romantic dinners at the elegant Broadmoor Resort. As the precious hours sped by, hearts were opened, tears were shed, hopes unveiled, and prayers offered. In the midst of spontaneous dancing and missing the Pikes Peak train, we were drawn into a camaraderie of connection and affection that lingers in our memory and unites us in shared experience.

INTIMACY AS A WAY OF LIFE

Our deepest human yearning is to be known, to be understood, to be loved and appreciated—and to know another with that same depth. This is why our American contemporary culture has so decimated the soul: because it has programmed us for superficiality. Busyness mandates superficiality. The "muchness and manyness" of our production-oriented mind-set multiplies this superficiality. The competition for corporate advancement and the consumption with obtaining wealth requires superficiality. We dare not risk intimacy, and even if we should be so inclined, we dare not waste the time!

So the dilemma grips us. We desire intimacy but are also deeply afraid of it. We want to connect in deep and lasting ways with people but are not sure how to do it. Or, more to the point, we don't know how to deprogram our subconscious motivations and engrained habits.

Be encouraged. This is a journey, after all. A baby step is still a step. Our awkward movements toward intimacy are steps toward the Kingdom of God and away from the world system with its controlling influences.

The "renewing of your mind" (Romans 12:2) is a process, and it begins with today's choices. Choose moments with God. Choose moments with your spouse. Choose moments with your son or daughter. Choose moments with your neighbor. People will always, always, always be more important than things! Always.

Shame and self-protection wall us off and truncate life down to a nub of its potential glory.

Why is intimacy scary? I think it is because we are often afraid of letting people see us as we really are; we are ashamed of who we sometimes are. We know our selfishness, we know our failures, and we know how people have hurt us before . . . and we are not anxious to go back there. So shame and self-protection wall us off from potential injury and with it the very fellowship and communion with others that is oxygen to our souls. We truncate life down to a nub of its potential glory—one missed opportunity at a time.

Our earthly life is a blend of joy and sorrow, of pain and delight, of failures and successes. When we attempt to isolate ourselves from suffering, we wind up shutting out the joys of life as well as the pain. Life is risky. Acceptance of risk allows us to embrace the adventure we were created for. Whether you're climbing a mountain, expanding your business, or falling in love—you cannot excel without becoming comfortable with risk.

As we learn to risk the pursuit of intimacy and cultivate its priority in our lives, we find ourselves increasingly capable of experiencing one of intimacy's vital outgrowths: community.

REACHING FOR COMMUNITY

Community has become something of a buzzword in recent years: in advertising, in neighborhoods, in clubs and churches, even in some corporate boardrooms. And thank God it has! We have endured a national famine of soul for the previous two generations, as the "builders" and "boomers" largely ignored community in their pursuit of security and material accumulation, respectively. Not everyone is guilty, of course, but these trends have put community on the endangered species list!

To a great degree it has taken the "Generation X-ers" to resurrect relationship as a driving motivational force. Assisting them has been the pendulum swing of a national soul, stuffed in a shoebox for decades and determined to reassert its legitimate appetite for togetherness.

But dare we take the plunge? Brennan Manning discloses our unspoken fears:

> Is there anyone I can level with? Anyone I dare tell that I am benevolent and malevolent, chaste and randy, compassionate and vindictive, selfless and selfish, that beneath my brave words lives a frightened child, that I dabble in religion and pornography, that I have blackened a friend's character, betrayed a trust, violated a confidence, that

I am tolerant and thoughtful, a bigot and a blowhard, that I hate hard rock?[1]

That level of honesty is terrifying in the extreme, and we have few role models to glean it from. The risks are real; therefore, it takes either extraordinary conviction or extraordinary pain to move us onto that playing field, to hesitantly unveil a fragment of our souls and anxiously await a response. Will we be embraced or excommunicated? We're not sure. We can only hope that finding a place of safety and communion will reward the effort.

We all long for a companion on this journey—someone to share our moments of blackness and brilliance. Someone to speak tender words of affirmation and someone to give us a kick in the pants. How we long—and how rarely we taste!

Community requires a common destination, a common affection, and a common trust.

Community requires that we have several things in common: a common destination, a common affection, and a common trust. If we are headed toward the same place, then we have *the opportunity* to walk together. If we care deeply for one another, then we have *the desire* to walk together. If we have experienced another's commitment to us in the storm, then we have *the confidence* to walk together.

But where are we headed, anyway? Does our destination have anything to do with our jobs, our training, our socioeconomics? Not much. It has to do with a Person. It has to do with pursuing the glimpses of eternal belonging we have found in Jesus. That experiential knowledge, that fellowship, is our destination—at least

I suspect it is for most of us. I have already contended in previous chapters that identity and purpose in life can only be known in the context of relationship. Subsequently, our destination is defined by relationship: *The* Relationship.

From there, our destinations diverge based upon our Kingdom passion: to pursue the revelation of God among the political and intellectual elite, to know Him and make Him known through the arts, to demonstrate the culture of heaven within the culture of today's business world. Each of these Kingdom destinations holds tremendous opportunity for true community!

But opportunity must be combined with a foundational respect of person and delight of personality. This base of mutual affection draws us together and implants the deep desire necessary to share our lives and reveal our true selves as we journey alongside each other.

Counselor and professor Dr. Dan Allendar paints a compelling picture toward an even higher quality of friendship in what he terms "the apostolic band"—in other words, a group of people living in community and called to a common mission:

> To join this apostolic band . . . I must cleave to this crew in the kind of relationship that invites others to fight, surrender, and party for a larger purpose than their own rights or pleasure. The result of leaving and cleaving will be a form of weaving, a union of souls that leads to greater playfulness, service, and worship. . . . We need a diverse group of people whose life stories, burdens, and training facilitate different aspects of disturbing, drawing, and directing others to Jesus.[2]

This caliber of friendship that develops among a small group of people about a common purpose gradually takes on the final, most crucial aspect of community: *a common trust.* Trust, unfortunately, only develops within the context of stress and difficulty, for it is in that setting that people reveal their true selves . . . and their true place within the community. Allendar amplifies:

> It is sacrifice, sorrow, and blood that bind the hearts of warriors and lovers together, not mere fraternity. . . . Cleaving is, in other words, not suburban, middle-class camaraderie built around free time, convenience, and a break from routine. . . . Cleaving in the war of life involves availability, responsibility, and accountability.[3]

Here it is that our romanticized notions of idealism in the journey are overwhelmed by the gut-wrenching pain of loss and disappointment as dreams are dashed, friends betray, and emotional props are shattered. In these moments we discover, perhaps to our surprise, who is committed to us with a love beyond affection and who lives for our good when the cost is high. Trust is the sweet fruit that falls from the branches of relationship shaken by storm.

My favorite movie of all time is *Braveheart*, a story based on the life of William Wallace. Behind the movie's guy-intoxicating blend of sweat and blood lie numerous depictions of some of life's greatest virtues and character. One of those is the quality of friendship enjoyed by Wallace and his two chief comrades. They enjoyed each other's company in times of peace, but it took going to war together to forge a bond that could not be broken. They protected one another's back, pulled out each other's arrows, mingled blood and tears, risked life and limb, and finally . . . when it was all over . . .

the two comrades watched William Wallace die. They lived the quality of community I want in my life.

Transparency and Accountability

As trust is established among those who struggle together in the trenches of service, two precious qualities emerge within the fellowship: *transparency* and *accountability*. The freedom to disclose one's heart with confidence multiplies the power of the community. Kellie calls it "coming into the open." The apostle John called it "walking in the light":

> God is light, pure light; there's not a trace of darkness in him.
>
> If we claim that we experience a shared life with him and continue to stumble around in the dark, we're obviously lying through our teeth—we're not *living* what we claim. But if we walk in the light, God himself being the light, we also experience a shared life with one another, as the sacrificed blood of Jesus, God's Son, purges all our sin. (1 John 1:5–7 MSG)

Kellie describes it this way: "When we choose to bring a temptation, sin, or frustration (anything that is having a negative effect on our lives) *into the open*—in other words, when we talk about it with someone we trust—the light of God floods that place in our lives, and healing comes. When we choose to keep hidden those places in our lives that are hurting us, then only Satan, darkness, and lies can take root.

"From our own experience," Kellie continues, "we are learning that when guilt and shame come to plague us, sharing those feelings with a trustworthy friend dispels the secrecy and power of the emotions. As long as we hide the pain, our enemy has the power to enforce those lies destructively in our minds and actions!"

Trust is the sweet fruit that falls from the branches of relationship shaken by storm.

I (Jerome) have already talked about realizing what a dearth of real friendships I had when we moved to Colorado. With few exceptions, I could only point to the *potential* friendships I had had in North Carolina, the opportunities for connection I had largely squandered. The relationships that had gone deeper had, in all honesty, been mostly initiated by others while I had been the more passive partner. However, as the light of my friendlessness has dawned, so my hunger for this very quality of community has grown proportionately.

James 5:16 urges us to confess our sins to one another. In my experience, this confessing does not come easily; it requires humility and honesty. But these are the very things that draw the heart of God to us (see James 4:6–8). And they are the same qualities that draw the hearts of friends together.

I discovered this truth recently after suffering the chronic shame of defiling dreams. As I multiplied prayer upon prayer, my frustration grew as I saw no lasting change to these nighttime oppressions. Occasionally I spoke of them to Kellie, asking for her prayers as well. But in this case, it wasn't until I took one further step and opened my heart up to several men for prayer and accountability that I received the freedom I sought. Then, in addition to my own freedom, I discovered that my vulnerability had other beneficial side effects: One of the men I shared with admitted his own struggle in the same arena, widening the circle of transparency and agreement. And among all those I opened up to, I found our friendships to be strengthened, not diminished, by the dynamic of my confession.

As the light of my friendlessness has dawned, so my hunger for community has grown proportionately.

On this subject, Dr. Allendar concurs: "Confession is an art of relationship that has been lost in our era [and it] is twofold: first, opening our heart to God, admitting we are far from home and need his grace, and then saying to the other what we have already said to God." Confession is the spiritual application of our honesty and transparency, both before God and men. But to clarify our understanding, Allendar continues,

> When we think of sojourning together for a common purpose, many Christians think only of "holding each other accountable"—making sure ("in love," of course) that everyone is doing their part for the kingdom. But accountability is not the process of chiding one another to be more faithful, nor is it merely encouraging others to be what they were meant to be. Rather, it is sitting back at the end of the day . . . , laughing . . . , teasing. . . . We are meant to weep together, marvel about each other, and with gratitude, let the sun set. Accountability means to recount the day together.[4]

Manning expands the quality of accountability among friends thus:

> Such a friend allows me to be myself, thoughtful one moment and silly the next. Between us, trust grows. If a word of fraternal correc-

tion is needed, the friend offers it directly, but the pained expression on his face tells me how difficult the reproof is for him. And yet he has the courage to tell me something unpleasant but necessary— something that others should tell me but do not. (They renege for fear that I will not like them anymore. Their emotional equilibrium is more important to them than my spiritual growth.)[5]

The feast of trust whets our appetite and beckons us toward its savory delight.

EMBARKING ON THE QUEST FOR FRIENDSHIP . . . AND COMMUNITY

Friendship, that possession the rich cannot buy and the poor cannot have repossessed, is in short supply these days, as trumpeted by book titles such as *The Friendless American Male*. Yet it lies within the grasp of each of us who have been changed from the inside out and now strive to reset our lives to orbit around relationship instead of production. Let's consider how to grasp this priceless possession, first by recognizing that although formulas fade in the light of relationship, we have some trustworthy guidelines from Solomon, a man who specifically asked God for wisdom and understanding and received . . .

- "A friend loves at all times, and a brother is born for adversity" (Proverbs 17:17). *Friendship perseveres through all storms and challenges.*

- "A man of many companions may come to ruin, but there is a friend who sticks closer than a brother" (Proverbs 18:24). *Focus friendship upon a worthy few.*

- "He who loves a pure heart and whose speech is gracious will have the king for his friend" (Proverbs 22:11). *When heart and words combine for another's good, friendship is felt.*

- "Wounds from a friend can be trusted, but an enemy multiplies kisses" (Proverbs 27:6). *Misunderstandings and offenses don't sink true friendship but rather strengthen it.*

- "Perfume and incense bring joy to the heart, and the pleasantness of one's friend springs from his earnest counsel" (Proverbs 27:9). *"Earnest counsel" conveys our commitment to a friend's welfare.*

Intimacy in friendship is, of course, the foundation upon which intimacy is cultivated in marriage, our next focus.

AND THEY WILL BECOME ONE FLESH

Kellie and I had a storybook romance, meeting in South Carolina on the campus of Columbia International University in late August 1990. Within a couple of days after arriving, I was introduced to Kellie by a mutual friend. Within a couple of weeks, we began hanging out together, running the loop around campus in the evenings—suddenly inspired with athletic endeavor. Jogging led to dates at Christian concerts and dinners at a popular restaurant, California Dreamin'. For Thanksgiving, I drove Kellie up to visit her sister in the mountains, although we didn't spend much time with the sister! I was smitten. And driving home, I composed a poem for my proposal. Being the patient sort, I waited all of three weeks to ask her father and then pop the question. In another dazzling display of temperance, we waited three months for a spring-break wedding. It was all a happy blur.

Five years later, we had a dawning realization that something fundamental in our marital foundation was awry. It came through a rediscovery of the ancient purpose statement for marriage given in Genesis:

For this reason a man will leave his father and mother and be united to his wife, and they will become one flesh. (Genesis 2:24)

I began to understand that I had never really "left" my parents and, because of that, had never been really free to "be united" with Kellie. Needless to say, our "one-flesh" unity had been elusive.

For five years the priority place in my heart, which rightfully belonged to Kellie, had been given instead to my father. And as good a man as he is, that fundamental misalignment had cost our marriage terribly. Upon this discovery, we attempted to repair the dynamics, but the unfortunate truth is that our fixes were superficial, and the root ailment remained for another four years . . . until our move to Colorado.

My experience—on both the receiving and the giving end of premarital counseling—is that this absolutely foundational declaration by God Himself in Genesis 2:24 is simply assumed and so is neglected as two young people eagerly prepare for a new life together. Within this brief verse we can find the keys to intimacy . . . intimacy with anyone, really, but certainly with a spouse! The goal of intimacy is oneness—a co-mingling of two that produces unity. And we learn the way that oneness is achieved is through a dual action: a leaving and

> *Needless to say, our "one-flesh" unity had been elusive.*

a uniting, or a "leaving and cleaving," to use the catchy King James language.

Oneness in Marriage

Marriage is our greatest human expression of this one-flesh miracle and a natural expansion on our topic of space in the home. Here the oneness God intends is pervasive—a united body, soul, and spirit forming where two individuals cease to exist as self-contained and self-determined. An entirely new composite is created. This new union forms its own intermingled personality, its own new meld of hopes and dreams, its unique calling and purpose as a united pair. One flesh.

Jimmy Evans unpacks this Genesis verse in brilliant fashion, uncovering four foundational principles in his book *Marriage on the Rock:* the law of priority, the law of pursuit, the law of possession, and the law of purity. With *priority,* we hold our spouse as the number one human relationship, protecting it from any challenger: against preoccupation with work, children, or other friendships. Through *pursuit,* we spend our absolute best time and energy working to increase the life and love of this precious union. In *possession,* we hold nothing to ourselves—not our bodies, not our money, not our time or attention—but jointly manage and cherish all we possess. And by *purity,* we recognize that our individual sin affects our spouse, so we are motivated toward complete transparency and repentance from our many failures.

Once we had settled into our Colorado home, Kellie and I began to explore Genesis 2:24 for our own marriage. In all honesty, it took an extended time with extensive work to repair the damage

I had inflicted for nine years and regain the lost trust. But our awesome Healer was faithful beyond belief; He redeemed our hearts and our souls, reuniting us in an enduring vision for unshakable oneness!

I would like to share here three components of that vision for oneness, with the hope that it will encourage those of you who are married to work toward that goal. If you are not married, you, too, will benefit from this vital discussion. Keep in mind that intimacy and space are kissing cousins; a lifestyle of space is the natural habitat of intimacy.

Merging in Moments. Someone has said that love is spelled t-i-m-e. Beyond the application of love languages, there is something heavenly for each of us about investing our most valuable resource in another person—our time. As it applies to marriage, I call this investment *merging in moments.* An atmosphere of space in the home allows you to pursue oneness by capturing moments of time. These moments are stolen away from insignificance, redeemed from triviality, and imbued with the power to unite two souls in one. Whether it is coming into agreeing prayer or processing the events of the day or stealing away to a romantic bed-and-breakfast, these are moments that merge us together and keep us from drifting apart. Oneness.

Merging in Mention. Another vital component is what I call *merging in mention.* Words have the power to take precious objects out of the closet of the soul and share them with another soul. Jesus said, "For out of the overflow of the heart the mouth speaks" (Matthew 12:34). This aspect of sharing life has not come easily for Kellie and me. Without any ill intent, we both find it easy to keep our thoughts to ourselves and unwittingly rob one another of the joys of verbal communion. The power of merging in mention allows us to enlarge one another and enlarge our union through communicating our thoughts of the day, our feelings of the moment, or our desires for the future. Part of my soul is transferred by the spoken word to Kellie's soul.

Let me offer an example. I was facing a financial crisis recently related to a business deal's being greatly delayed. It had been weighing on me for weeks, and of course Kellie knew about it. But one day I felt like I should break out of my own mental gymnastics and talk it through with her, so we sat down as I began to rehearse what I was feeling. As I vented a host of emotions, several amazing things began to happen.

Words have the power to take precious objects out of the closet of the soul and share them with another soul.

First, I began to realize that my anxiety was not so much bound up in the finances but in a relationship that was being strained in the process. Second, Kellie had the insight to urge me to call the person that day and clear the air. Finally, and most importantly, our own connection was strengthened by what my father calls "touching the same thing." Understanding, wisdom, fellowship—all these needed functions were released by *merging in mention.*

More intimacy. More oneness.

Merging in Ministry. Many couples involved in church ministry divide their focus. He does worship, and she does women. Or he helps with stewardship, and she helps with children. *Merging in ministry* is different. It allows us to combine our spiritual gifts in synergistic potency for advancing the Kingdom of God in our sphere.

Certainly we bring different giftings to the union, and sometimes those giftings will be applied individually. But the goal lies in being fully vested in your spouse's realm of ministry and looking for every opportunity to converge your gifts into the same context.

At this point in our ministry, I am the one who's writing this book. But Kellie and I are truly partnering in its creation. She is much more than merely a support and encouragement to "my ministry"; there is an active mutuality in the formation of thought and expression that winds up on the pages I type. Thus the title of "oneFlesh Ministries." Oneness is our theme in life; intimacy is our goal.

THE DIVINE UNION

While the Genesis 2:24 pattern of leaving and uniting for the purpose of intimacy has a rather matter-of-fact application to marriage, Paul did something extraordinary with it: He dangerously applied this same pattern to our relationship with God Himself. Ephesians 5:31–32 picks up the Genesis reference and runs with it:

> For this reason a man will leave his father and mother and be united to his wife, and the two will become one flesh. This is a profound mystery—but I am talking about Christ and the church.

What?! Christ and the church becoming one flesh? You and I are . . . destined to "marry" Christ? Mind-boggling but absolutely true. This entire passage on how wives and husbands should relate is interwoven with this same analogy:

- "Husbands, love your wives, just as Christ loved the church" (5:25).

- "[Christ] gave himself up for [the church], to make her holy. . . . In this same way, husbands ought to love their wives as their own bodies" (5:25, 28).

- "No [husband] ever hated his own body, but he feeds and cares for it, just as Christ does the church" (5:29).

And at the very end of the Book, the Lamb (Jesus) is preparing for an elaborate feast and ceremony to wed His bride, the church (see Revelation 19:7–9, 21:2–10, and 22:16–17).

Okay, that's all very nice in a literary sort of way, you're probably thinking, *but what does it mean for me?*

It means the unthinkable—that the God of glory, whose awesomeness cannot even be looked upon by humankind, the magnificent, infinite One who is beyond time and space, who reclines upon the galaxies and uses earth as an ottoman—this unapproachable Light has approached us with enraptured delight and eternal intent!

The most glorious human marriage is but a shadow and hint of God's design for His intimacy with you and me. If this idea is hard to get a handle on, then good—you are on the right track!

One thing, however, we know: Intimacy with God requires the same leaving and uniting that a marriage does. What do we leave? In a nutshell, we leave the very world system we have spent so much time trying to understand: We leave the root sins of pride, fear, and greed; we leave the heart motivations of insecurity, materialism, and control; and we definitely leave behind the soul clutter of drivenness, distraction, and superficiality. We leave these old false lovers, and we unite ourselves to God through priority, pursuit, possession, and purity. He becomes our passion, our magnificent obsession.

A startling statement from Jack Deere has become a personal banner for my life: *I have made a commitment to subordinate everything in my life to the pursuit of intimacy with God.*[6] The hope for and the emerging reality of friendship with God overarches my days with desire and delight. It has made some of the Psalms come freshly alive with meaning:

> One thing I ask of the LORD, this is what I seek: that I may dwell in the house of the LORD all the days of my life, to gaze upon the beauty of the LORD and to seek him in his temple. (Psalm 27:4)

> Better is one day in your courts than a thousand elsewhere; I would rather be a doorkeeper in the house of my God than dwell in the tents of the wicked. (Psalm 84:10)

If you ask me what intimacy with God fully entails, I can't answer you. But I want to spend my life finding out and the sum of my life to bear reply. Surely this is what we are made for—all of us! Whether programmer or paralegal, plumber or politician, our overriding purpose is to know Him and to make Him known. It's the ultimate for any of us.

THE INESCAPABLE ISSUE

So you want to deepen your relationships, but you're not sure how to do it. The magnetic force of all these discussions tends to pull us back to *the inescapable issue of time and how we use it:* A surprise getaway weekend with your husband. Rock climbing with your son. A spontaneous trip to visit your aging grandfather. A phone call to your cousin on the other coast. Rediscovering family reunions (maybe even organizing one!). Pulling together a group of guys to go mountain biking every Wednesday after work . . . then taking time after the ride to navigate the more uncertain paths of each other's hearts.

Let's be honest. None of this stuff is terribly complicated. It just takes vision married to effort. It's like someone has observed about prayer: The only way to fail is to not show up! The key to deepening our experience of intimacy in relationships is simply to show up—to show up emotionally, that is. To show up with interest and attention. With intention. Show up by asking real questions, like "What are your dreams in life?" "What are your memories as a child?" "What are you most afraid of?"

This unapproachable Light has approached us with enraptured delight and eternal intent!

Take the risk to probe. Search. Draw out a person's deep heart. As Solomon counseled, "The purposes of a man's heart are deep waters, but a man of understanding draws them out" (Proverbs 20:5).

Just figuring out that our hearts can only thrive within a context of community, and really believing it, is the largest hurdle. But the fact that you have read this far shows that you are hungry and thirsty for this quality of life. As the old commercial said, *Obey your thirst!*

SOULSPACE PRESCRIPTION

Make a list of three people you know who have the capacity for much greater friendship with you than you now experience. Think of what kind of time together would best enhance those relationships (a phone call, an activity, a lunch, a trip), and put it tentatively on your calendar right now. Then go about making it happen.

chapter nine

A Recipe for Energy—
and Rest

The energetic dynamics of clutter are often related to issues that you hide away and don't want to deal with. Clutter creates creativity obstacles in our lives. It helps to slow us down, sabotage our dreams, and throw a monkey wrench into the workings of the "divine order."

—NANCY SANTOPIETRO

I WAS MEETING MY LONGTIME FRIEND Jeff down in Florida at Disney's Epcot Center for a guy weekend some years ago. He lived near Orlando, and we needed little excuse to indulge our "inner child" with the tantalizing sights, smells, and experiences of this wonderland. Upon checking in to the aquatic-themed Dolphin Hotel, we plunged into the global village of Epcot with passion—tasting the exotic foods, browsing the endless markets, and soaking in the visual extravaganza of the various countries represented.

Maybe four hours later, lunch was starting to settle, the temperature was warming up, and my senses were on overload. Somewhat embarrassed, I had to admit to myself and to Jeff that I was drained—physically and emotionally exhausted. A slim, fit, thirty-something guy, I had petered out after half of our first day. *Pitiful,* I thought.

THE LINK BETWEEN ENERGY AND SOULSPACE

Energy is one more reality that affects our entire beings: body, soul, and spirit. Physical energy, which I had in short supply that day in Orlando, is a reality we easily relate to. Some days we feel boundless energy, perhaps on a crisp fall day as summer's humid oppression fades and the leaves begin to glow with color. We want to run instead of walk, kick piles of leaves, hike mountain paths, and feel the rush of air as our bikes hurtle down a trail. Other days . . . well, we don't even want to push our feet over the edge of the bed. Our legs feel too heavy to walk across the room, our motions are drugged and painful. On these mornings it requires intense concentration to pour a bowl of cereal, and getting up to find a napkin isn't worth the effort.

Soul energy, or emotional energy, ebbs and surges in the same way. Some days are a rush of creative thought and inspiration: We write letters with flair, tackle a new project with confidence, and feel empowered to change the world. We dream, and we do. We are cheerful and positive, and we spread that energy to those around us. In contrast, when our emotional energy is depleted, we are quite the opposite: Instead of creating life, we suck it out of all those souls unfortunate enough to be in proximity to us that day.

Of course physical and soul energy are connected. When we're depressed or discouraged, our plunging emotional level usually manifests itself quickly in a lack of physical energy and motivation. Conversely, when we are injured or sick, it is very difficult to be "up" emotionally. In these situations all soul energy is turned inward, focused on healing and recovery. And then there's PMS . . . enough said.

Although we are not always so attuned to its dynamics, spiritual energy works in the same ways. Most of us have experienced the positive spiritual energy of certain moments or places: an intensity of worship, a riveting drama, a concert that entranced—something that superceded emotional excitement and moved us spiritually toward union, toward connection, with God. Perhaps it showed up as reverential awe, perhaps as tears, perhaps as a sacred sense of space, perhaps as wild, noisy dance! On the other hand, we've all tasted negative spiritual energy: a terror-filled nightmare, a location that felt inexplicably dark, a person who seemed intimidating or sinister.

> *We act and interact with others and within ourselves, being refreshed and depleted over time.*

So what does all this energy talk have to do with soulspace? Quite a lot, actually. In this chapter, I want to offer some important tools for managing space in your life through understanding Kingdom resources—the energy of the soul and the virtue of rest. These are facets of soulcare that do not receive enough attention in most Christian circles but are vital to building God-centered, soul-healthy lives.

The Battle Against "Digitosis"

Without getting deeply metaphysical, there is a pretty common-sense explanation for energy. As humans created with a body, soul, and spirit, we ebb and flow with resources—we give out, and we take in. We act and interact with others and within ourselves, enlarging and diminishing, being refreshed and being depleted in our souls over time.

Here's an example: Everything has gone digital now—watches, music, cell phones, TVs, you name it. *Digital* has become synonymous with "new" and "better"; the word represents advances in technology that improve the quality of life for us all. Well, uh . . . maybe.

Anti-technology I am not. As a musician, I have great appreciation for high-fidelity music. As a movie buff, I enjoy high-definition video. As a recovering gadget person, I am drawn by mind control to anything that has lights and knobs. However, my experience is that technology often *takes* more than it *gives*. My opinion is that for a gadget to earn its right to exist in my domain, it should give back more than I put in.

While many would disagree with me (and obviously do, based upon the current technology feeding frenzy), I found that my cool little palm-sized computer—you know, the kind that stores addresses, notes, and other essential information electronically—was a taker, not a giver. I spent more time programming it, charging its batteries, and trying to recover lost data than I ever did with paper organizers. So I gave it away.

Ahhhh . . . space!

Now, I'm not saying I've sworn off all means of electronic communicating, data storage, and word processing. I use e-mail daily. And as a writer, I rely heavily upon my computer. But I've found that I must guard against being consumed by these space-age devices, because spending too much time with them can lead to a disease I call "digitosis." This condition is a deterioration of the soul caused by a mindless love affair with technology for its own sake, an indiscriminate absorption in new distractions without careful analysis of their impact upon our quality of life and health of soul.

I am not advocating a Thoreau-like renunciation of civilization, but I would call for a thoughtful, patient, and somewhat skeptical approach to all the marketing hype surrounding emerging technology. The test for technology, or other materials seeking a place in our lives, is asking, How does it affect my soul energy?

KNOW THYSELF

We have established that our souls take in and give out, are refreshed and depleted in energy for thinking, energy for feeling, and energy for willing. To be honest, some relationships and activities are important in our lives even though we function strictly in the role of giver; but even then we need to at least understand what is taking place. If we wish to manage our souls well and sustain their lasting health, it is imperative that we learn to evaluate our level of spiritual energy and to regularly tend our souls with an eye toward renewed energy. Truly, soulcare is essential to spiritual health.

My energy crash in Orlando that day was not brought on by lack of physical conditioning. I have discovered about myself that I am a very simple person. While some seem to thrive on chaotic activity and are able to endlessly multitask, I get easily overloaded with too much information and quickly depleted by emotional overstimulation. Having slowly come to terms with this in myself, I am able to compensate for my own limitations and protect myself from draining all my reserves. The principle is the same when applied to the energy of the soul: No matter what your own personal capacity is, learn what energizes you and what de-energizes you so you can maintain your space! We must take in more than we put out, in body, soul, and spirit, to retain a positive energy balance.

Are you starting to see how energy fits into the "big picture" of soulspace? Solitude and prayer create space for renewing energy in our minds, our emotions, and our desires whereas clutter depletes it. Healthy relationships within a community have the potential to renew our soul energy whereas dysfunctional relationships drain energy. Clarity of identity and purpose renews energy; confusion and diffusion sap it away. A peaceful environment within the home restores the soul that has been sucked dry during a stressful day; a family in constant conflict ravages the depleted soul and drives it further from its true calling and destiny.

> *Ignorance kills our souls a day at a time while vigilance nurtures our souls a day at a time.*

Contrary to the old motto, ignorance is *not* bliss. Ignorance kills our souls a day at a time while vigilance nurtures our souls a day at a time. We must cultivate awareness of our condition so that we know when to forge ahead and when to withdraw. We must hone our skills of discernment and not be programmed by common assumptions. Instead of letting our culture set the pace, we must lay hold of the reins of our own souls and govern them wisely.

What things energize you, either physically or emotionally? What de-energizes you? What activities or environments have the ability to renew or deplete you? You need to know! Crowds of people invigorate some but drain others. You might be one who is energized by reading and study, by the pursuit of knowledge and the stimulation of creative thinking . . . or those activities may leave you cold. Instead you might find soul refreshment in a nature hike on a beautiful day. Strangely, both choices are true of me. In this context Socrates' admonition to "know thyself" is not as humanistic as is sometimes thought!

If this discussion sounds self-centered and secular, I would urge you to reconsider. Ask yourself—*When my body is beyond exhaustion, can I effectively fellowship with God and hear His voice? When my soul is isolated and starved for relationship, am I inclined to serve others with grace and compassion?*

The topic of stewardship played a vital role in the teachings of Christ, and though His teachings are most commonly applied to physical wealth, they also describe the way we're to use the resources of our bodies and souls. Both the Gospels of Matthew and Luke record the parable of the talents, or *minas*. The point of Jesus' story was to impress upon His followers the importance of caring well for what had been entrusted to their keeping. He taught the significance of watchfulness and faithfulness in the parable of the ten virgins (see Matthew 25:1–13), where five took their stewardship seriously and five did not, with devastating consequence. Jesus' parable of the sower (see Matthew 13:18–23) is also focused upon rightly stewarding the revelation of God. I have come to the conviction that maintaining right reserves of energy in my life is a key requisite to fulfilling my Kingdom purpose in this world.

RECLAIMING KINGDOM RESOURCES

Some years back I was greatly impressed with the power of two things to further the Kingdom of God or, conversely, the kingdoms of this world: time and money. While neither of these things is inherently spiritual, nothing so honestly reveals the values and intentions of our hearts as an evaluation of our *checkbooks* and our *schedules*!

The investment of our money and our time displays, not the mission statement printed on our letterhead, but the actual mission statement of our lives. It is the quickest reality check upon our tendency for self-deception and our habit of judging others by their actions but ourselves by our intentions. Money, particularly, is a complex topic and one that received extensive attention from Jesus, who taught His followers about its dangers, responsibilities, and power.

> *Nothing so honestly reveals the values of our hearts as an evaluation of our* checkbooks *and our* schedules!

Both time and money are entrusted to us in order to express and advance the cause of Christ in the earth—to impress the patterns and Presence of heaven upon the fabric of our lives, our families, our communities, and our planet.

Kellie and I felt a definite rub about taking such a large amount of both time and money to pull off our sabbatical year. Even though our friends were very supportive, and even though we knew that what we were doing was aimed at the restoration of our souls, we felt undercurrents of disapproval at times as we swam against the tide of normal practice. But in our own hearts it was more than worth the cost of selling a car and a house to finance the kind of transformation we were experiencing! The Kingdom realignment in our lives has been, quite simply, priceless. So using the energy and resources at our disposal to lay hold of these eternal treasures felt like the greatest level of stewardship we knew.

If sustaining the energy and health of our souls is essential to our heavenly calling—and I have offered many reasons in this book why I believe it is—then it follows that time and money spent in the renewal of our souls (as well as of those in our sphere of influence) are time and money well spent! Jesus Himself questioned rhetorically, "What good will it be for a man if he gains the whole world, yet forfeits his soul? Or what can a man give in exchange for his soul?" (Matthew 16:26).

If I could expand upon Jesus' words, I would put it this way: What good is it for a businesswoman to float a multimillion-dollar initial public offering of stock that gives 10 percent to fund world missions—but to neglect her own soul and thus never experience personal intimacy with God? Or, what Kingdom purpose is really served when a pastor builds a magnificent church organization that becomes the national model for newly planted churches—but neglects his own marriage and doesn't know his children?

Don't think that the word *soul* in Jesus' question above referred to "getting saved." Jesus was addressing Peter, who was quite "saved" but whose mind was filled with the world system's expectation that Jesus must become an earthly king. In the strongest rebuke that ever fell from His lips, Jesus definitively declared that no religious regime could compare to the Kingdom power of keeping one's own soul secured in its true identity and released in its true calling.

THE CASE FOR SIMPLICITY

In my pursuit of God through a lifestyle of space, I am discovering how to apply the power of simplicity to my reserves of spiritual energy as well as to sharpen my identity and my calling. This is not a new discovery. Many persons, both Christians and others, have walked this path through past centuries and have felt its power to free the soul from its Adam-led pull toward clutter and diffusion.

Let me offer some practical examples: I have discovered that reading the newspaper leaves me feeling emotionally and physically drained. (Stop laughing at me!) So, I no longer subscribe to a daily paper. For me, that's a no-brainer! It's an absurdly simple example, but it raises a couple of pointedly personal questions: How well do we monitor our souls, and how willing are we to cut across cultural norms in order to facilitate our own souls' health?

Here's another example: I get wonderful renewal from the outdoors. This has always been true since I was a young kid spending my summers exploring creeks and building forts, but I almost entirely lost contact with this fact upon entering the "real world" of work and ministry. Even now I sometimes have to tear myself away from the computer—from my passion and calling to write—in order to manage my soul

Selah

will rejuvenate our worship and transform all of life into worship!

well and refresh myself so as to protect my passion and calling. I find that refreshment through a bike ride, or rock climbing, or even walking down my long driveway.

Beyond our choice of activities and environment, the pace of life we set for ourselves remains a defining factor. Busyness inevitably drains, whereas rest restores. That doesn't mean we should never be busy. On the contrary, the value of rest and restoration presumes that we have spent our energy in good and legitimate endeavors. Yet what pervades our culture is a Kingdomadverse addiction to expenditure and production with scant attention paid to renewal.

There is a deafening silence in contemporary Christian teaching regarding the role of pausing in our everyday work to enjoy stillness, peace, and rest. But when we peruse biblical teaching, we find them to be extensive themes related to God's intention toward His people.

For starters, there is the mysterious term *selah* sprinkled liberally throughout the Psalms (seventy-one times, to be exact). Although the term itself is surrounded by interpretational uncertainty, the consensus is that it indicates a "musical or liturgical interlude,"[1] a "suspension or pause."[2] Some commentators believe the author of these psalms applied the word "to direct the singer to be silent, or to pause a little, while the instruments played an interlude."[3] Others surmise it to mean "let the singer meditate while the music stops."[4] These descriptions give us a pretty good idea that, however it may have been technically applied by the ancient musicians, the practice of pausing was essential to the Davidic model of worship. And so it is to ours. To pause is to rein in our action for a moment, to wait rather than plunge ahead, to consider—in the context of worship—the testament of our words and our very lives.

From studying this strategic choice of word and concept, I believe this kind of silent reflection is an important part of rightly understanding and worshiping God. We might even say that *soul-space* is a modern term for the ancient idea of *selah*. One wonders whether David would have had the ability to plumb the depths of God as he did, much less express them in eloquent poetry and song, without large and frequent doses of soulspace! Should we expect to touch the heart of God as this warrior worshiper did without utilizing the simple means he used?

If we want to follow David's example, how can we implement a *selah* lifestyle in today's world? The answer lies in practicing some of the very skills we have studied in relation to soulspace: prayer, solitude, study of motivations, reflection, the loving challenge of friends, renewal of energy, etc. At the least, *selah* will rejuvenate our worship of God; at the most, *selah* will transform all of life into worship!

The Sacred Stillness of God

Beyond the mere word *selah,* many of the psalms themselves describe a soul that finds a home of space in the sacred stillness of God:

- "I have stilled and quieted my soul; like a weaned child with its mother, like a weaned child is my soul within me" (131:2).

- "My soul finds rest in God alone; my salvation comes from him" (62:1).

- "Be still, and know that I am God" (46:10).

- "He who dwells in the shelter of the Most High will rest in the shadow of the Almighty. I will say of the LORD, 'He is my refuge and my fortress, my God, in whom I trust'" (91:1–2).

- "Even the sparrow has found a home, and the swallow a nest for herself, where she may have her young—a place near your altar. . . . Blessed are those who dwell in your house; they are ever praising you" (84:3–4).

An Essential Peace

Similar themes pervade the Scriptures beyond the Psalms. For example, the emphasis on *peace* is a telling one. Jesus was prophesied by Isaiah as the "Prince of Peace" (Isaiah 9:6), and peace is cited as a fruit of the Holy Spirit (see Galatians 5:22). Even the Jewish greeting *shalom* is a rich blessing of peace. This peace is an essential part of soulspace, a part that many of us would admit is not descriptive of our current lives.

Finding regular venues of peace in our lives is essential to rightly stewarding our souls. For the almost nine years Kellie and I have had children, we've found only two reliable times of peace within our home: before they get up and after they go to bed! We try to capture those precious moments and use them wisely. Of course, the waking moments are precious, too . . . just not often peaceful! Kellie and I have also adopted the practice of giving one another a "prayer day" during most weeks. We've learned that, in addition to the power of prayer itself, there is a tremendous power of renewal simply in getting outside our normal routines to a place of inner and outer quietness—a place of peace.

The Redemption of Rest

Rest is another biblical theme that influences a right understanding of energy and space. Rest was significant enough for God Himself to establish one entire day out of seven devoted to it alone. Since God doesn't exactly get tired, it is apparent that He was making a statement and establishing an important precedent for the human race right from its infancy. Not only is God seeking to restrain our own proclivities toward a destructive pace of busyness, He is revealing to us that rest is a characteristic of His Kingdom, as is work.

We'll discuss the Sabbath further in the following chapter. For now, let me simply point out that God's emphasis upon rest didn't end with the Sabbath. The establishment of Israel in the Promised Land is an illustration of how God brings us into Kingdom living. Everything from defeating our sin to discovering our life purpose to entering heaven itself is reflected in Israel's long campaign to leave Egypt, cross the desert, and occupy Canaan. Out of the desert of our lives, God's purpose is to give us a "land flowing with milk and honey"!

In Exodus 33:1, 14, God calls Moses to lead His people to this Promised Land, and He specifically describes that land using the word *rest*:

> Then the LORD said to Moses, "Leave this place, you and the people you brought up out of Egypt, and go up to the land I promised on oath to Abraham, Isaac and Jacob, saying, 'I will give it to your descendants.'" . . . The LORD replied, "My Presence will go with you, and I will give you *rest*." (Emphasis added.)

The directive is confirmed again in Deuteronomy 12:10, contrasted in Psalm 95:8–11, and echoed by Jesus in Matthew 11:28. Later, two entire chapters (3 and 4) in Hebrews are devoted to comparing Joshua and Moses' leading the Israelites into rest with Jesus' leading us into an even greater rest. A passage in chapter 4 clarifies that the occupation of Canaan foreshadowed the rest to come through Christ:

For if Joshua had given them rest, God would not have spoken later about another day. There remains, then, a Sabbath-rest for the people of God; for anyone who enters God's rest also rests from his own work, just as God did from his. Let us, therefore, make every effort to enter that rest. (vv. 8–11)

Because of Jesus' sacrifice on the cross, once for all, we can finally cease our futile attempts to earn our own salvation and *rest* in what Christ has accomplished for us. But this rest is not limited to our initial salvation! Just as grace forms not only the basis for our first saving encounter with God but also the daily lives we live, so the quality of divine rest supercedes "getting saved" and infuses every moment of our lives with the liberating fragrance of heaven.

Cultivating Restfulness in Mind and Heart

Rest applies to our entire beings—body, mind, emotions, will, and spirit. Rest of spirit involves our salvation, both our initial entry into the Kingdom and our daily life in the Kingdom, as we just discussed. Outside of the spirit-rest Jesus won for us, we have no basis or reasonable hope for soul-rest. If it were not for the cross of Christ that gifted us with undeserved spiritual rest, we would have little ability for carving out our rest of soul in day-to-day living.

A vision for soul-rest moves us into living out our salvation in the most practical ways. The pressure is off! We don't have to labor and struggle to climb the corporate ladder; we don't have to earn our value by doing more than everyone else. We can cultivate a restfulness of mind and heart that is far from laziness but is all about renewing our energies in order to spend them upon our true callings. We rest our wills by taking a Sabbath and by restraining our greed and spending. We rest our minds by limiting the amount of information coming into the house and by focusing our attention upon things that have value and substance. We rest our emotions through prayer, solitude, and fellowship.

This principle of rest carries over into the physical realm, where we resist the allure of burning the midnight oil and struggling to beat the system; instead, we embrace sleep as the gift of God, the reward for those who have labored well during the day. I remember times when I would mutter my frustration with the seeming constriction of having only twenty-four hours in a day—as if I were smarter than God. I was disgruntled particularly that I couldn't operate on six hours of sleep a night like some people I knew.

The truth of Psalm 127:2 was a refreshing discovery: "In vain you rise early and stay up late, toiling for food to eat—for he grants sleep to those he loves." Sleep is a reward to be gratefully received and cherished instead of resisted or neglected. There can be little dispute that physical rest sets up the mind, emotions, and will to be their best so we can engage our work with passion and power for the glory of God and the advancement of His Kingdom.

SOULSPACE PRESCRIPTION

Think right now of one activity that de-energizes you and make a solid decision to limit its effect upon your soulspace in a tangible way. Next, identify one energizing activity and make a commitment to implement it into each week of the coming month.

chapter ten

Reworking
Your Workspace

The first thing revealed about God in the Bible is that he is the Creator and that he created by speaking into darkness. . . . Could it be that God intended [us] to behave like him by courageously moving into whatever spheres of mystery [we] encounter and speaking with imagination and life-giving power into the confusion [we] face?

—DR. LARRY CRABB

A CLOSE FRIEND OF MINE is a graphic artist who spent five years working for a graphics company before launching out to start his own business. During those years as an employee, he set an impressive example of infusing his work environment with space. Much to the perplexity of his co-workers, David's practice was to take his lunch hour at home every day with his family instead of joining the crowd headed out to the local grill. In addition, from day one, he committed to be out the door by 5:30 sharp—on his way home to enjoy his wife and four kids and invest himself in what was really important! He set this as a boundary with his boss the day he was hired and never deviated from it, even when pressured to do so.

God's blessings were evident in that this friend never missed a deadline and managed over time to earn the grudging respect of his boss and peers while maintaining a consistent influence for

Christ in his office environment. The curious uniqueness of his priorities, the polite behavior of his children at office parties, and the high caliber of his work all combined to give David many opportunities over the years to communicate the spiritual center of his life. In his determination to protect the priority of his home, he even turned down promotions that would have required more time in the office. To me, David is a rare and wonderful model of pursuing one's calling with excellence while staying focused on the real treasures in life!

I have used a large number of words in this book to describe the dangers of becoming consumed by work, of being lost in the pursuit of production, and of seeking validation through what we can accomplish. In the face of America's epidemic with clutter, I don't regret a single one of those words. And so far I have not attempted to express a "balanced" perspective on work; rather, I have sought to counter the extreme imbalance I perceive around me daily.

Now, however, I wish to affirm the high value of work and set it in its proper Kingdom context. I stated in the last chapter that both rest and work are Kingdom virtues, and in this chapter I want to describe some of the lessons Kellie and I have learned about shaping our work worlds with heavenly vision.

One of my great delights is waking up in the morning looking forward to my work that day. With rare exception, I can't wait to jump on my computer and begin to write or prepare for a worship or a teaching event. But it wasn't always that way! I remember my first job out of college working for a bank as a loan officer. After the first months of novelty wore off, I became more and more bored with it all and began to live for the weekends and to dread Monday mornings. But more disturbing than that was the growing awareness that almost everyone who worked there felt the same way. In fact, there was an underlying assumption around me that work was by definition tedious and distasteful, that weekdays were to be grudgingly tolerated in order to enjoy a few hours' play on the weekends.

"Not *my* life!" I wanted to scream. "I was born for more than this!" I left the bank at my first opportunity two years later, knowing I was born for a purpose. And so are you!

A HEAVENLY PATTERN

At the creation of the world, God set Adam in the garden He had made with a mission: "to work it and take care of it" (Genesis 2:15). Living in this paradise, Adam learned the role of work in God's original intention—a pattern that he had difficulty carrying over into his post-fall labors when the natural world began to resist him. And this is our challenge as well, a difficult but attainable quest to live out "your kingdom come, your will be done on earth as it is in heaven" (Matthew 6:10) in the workplace. It will never be fully heaven on earth until Christ accomplishes that very thing, but our task, in both prayer and life, is to reach into heaven, as it were, and draw out the eternal qualities of God, infusing our labor and relationships with these heavenly deposits!

WORKING IN PARTNERSHIP WITH GOD

What we see about Adam, first day on the job, is that he is *working in partnership.* "Pop" built the store and then invited His son to run it. The garden was not created to be self-sustaining, even in Eden;

instead, God created something that required a holy partnership between the divine and the human.

And so it goes for us today. Whether we are attorneys, bookkeepers, or homebuilders, God's intention is that we enter into partnership with Him around work that has Kingdom value. For example, if you're an attorney, a bookkeeper, or a homebuilder, then you can work toward the Kingdom value of justice, stewardship, or shelter. If you're not sure that your work has eternal value, then one of two things is true: Either you're not looking at it with Kingdom eyes, or it truly lacks eternal value in your life. If the former is the case, you need to ask God for His perspective on your labor; if it's the latter, you need to look for different work!

The opportunity for all of us is to enjoy a tangible sense of partnership and camaraderie with God Himself.

The desire of our heavenly Father throughout all human history has been for a special fellowship with us, His children—a fellowship in work and a fellowship in rest. The opportunity for all of us, even in the most monotonous of tasks, is to enjoy a tangible sense of partnership and camaraderie with God Himself as we work. That is a "kingdom come" experience, one I enjoy most days. Most of the time I get out of bed with an inner excitement about joining God in the work of my day. Work is meant to be part of a story that's bigger than our own; it's intended as part of God's story!

Working Our Passion

The second part of God's pattern for our work is that we *work our passion*. We were not created as homogenous workhorses, to have our lives' pursuits defined by the market forces of supply and demand. Rather, we were each created for a very specific purpose, assigned a collection of unique talents and passions, and released into the world to find a way to express those holy designs.

Yes, I know that is a very idealistic view that has numerous practical challenges. I know gifted artists who cannot live off their art. My friend Paul is gifted with the high calling of teaching but could not support his family with the ridiculously low wages paid to public schoolteachers and so had to make a career change. Most of us have secret dreams of what we wish we could do and make a decent living from it.

Here are my thoughts on how you can work toward that goal. *First,* know what you were made for. Search out your spiritual gifts, your natural abilities, your sense of divine purpose, and keep it always before you.

Second, keep moving toward work that releases your true purpose; don't become complacent with something that pays the bills but doesn't satisfy.

Third, don't throw away your dreams. God plants desires within us for a reason and calls us to pursue the divine partnership across challenge and risk. It may take months, years, or decades to obtain that true fit into the work we were fashioned for, but it is worth the journey.

Fourth, don't settle. As much as I enjoyed most aspects of being a worship pastor, I began to see how it was actually a hindrance to other important callings upon my life. So instead of settling for a secure place and a partially fulfilled calling, I had to take a risky leap to find a work setting that better facilitated the purpose of God on my life. I am carving out that space now.

As an aside, the power of partnership is multiplied when God brings us together with one or two or a few others with similar callings, and the "apostolic band" is released into its fellowship and function. In addition, God occasionally allows a husband and wife the special privilege of partnering in work as well as the home. That is a deep joy for Kellie and me.

Working with Space

A third part of God's pattern for work is to *work with space,* applying the principles of space that have been shared throughout this book to the world of work as much as you have opportunity to do so. We'll examine this important part of the pattern in more detail later in the section titled "Work Your Space."

Knowing When to Stop

A final piece to a heavenly pattern of work is simply *knowing when to stop!* The Sabbath principle has been so greatly neglected in contemporary society over the past few generations that it is now usually viewed as a quaint, odd practice . . . when it's considered at all. Even in the church, where we might expect this ancient commandment to thrive, we see instead that people frequently build their work worlds upon the foundation of shifting cultural currents rather than upon God's established wisdom.

Why in the world would God, in His top-ten list of the most fundamental behavioral truths for all time—right there amidst "do not murder" and "do not make for yourself an idol" (my translation, Exodus 20:4, 13)—why would he include "remember the Sabbath" (Exodus 20:8)? Indeed, of all the Ten Commandments, God spent more time describing this one than any of the others. Could it be that this need for rest is as essential to rightly stewarding the image of God in ourselves as it is for us to respect the image of God in another person by not committing murder? Apparently so.

At the root of Sabbath-keeping lies a deep humility—the recognition and declaration that I cannot do it all, that I am not supposed to do it all, that God is God and I am not. Conversely, at the heart of frantic busyness and our subsequent soul clutter lies an incredible arrogance. "To act as if the world cannot get along without our work for one day in seven is a startling display of pride that denies the sufficiency of our generous Maker," declares Dorothy Bass. "When Sabbath comes," she continues, "commerce halts, feasts are served, and all God's children play."[1]

> *At the root of Sabbath-keeping lies a deep humility—the recognition that I cannot do it all.*

According to Jewish liturgy, "The holiness of the Sabbath is also made manifest in the joy people expect to experience on that day. It is a good deed for married couples to have sexual intercourse on *Shabbat*. Taking a walk, resting, talking with loved ones, reading—these are good, too. . . . Not good are work and commerce and worry."[2]

Many wonderful things could be said about the theological and practical virtues of Sabbath-keeping—the celebration of resurrection and communion, the historical and cultural applications, the psychological benefits, the opportunities to worship and serve—but it is all summed up in the theme of rest. And so rest becomes the antidote to our bondage of will, liberating us from the harsh taskmaster of "muchness and manyness" (Richard Foster's term) into a life-giving space of will, a will we then offer to God Himself in Sabbath worship and to our spouses, families, and friends in Sabbath refreshment.

I received many wonderful foundations in my life from the instruction of my parents, among them a love for worship, a value for tithing, and a pattern of Sabbath-keeping. Throughout nineteen years of schooling, the habit was ingrained in me that study was prohibited on Sundays. And although I periodically chafed at the restriction, the further I went, the more I began to value the freedom of having a day's rest each week—a day when my soul could be refreshed, when the soil of my mind could lie dormant for twenty-four hours and so return with fresh vigor on Monday.

Like so many of God's commandments, this one is sometimes caricatured as evidence of God's anti-fun, uptight religiosity; as a result, people miss God's intention to bless us, knowing we aren't smart enough to set beneficial boundaries for ourselves. I have come to believe that if we were to only catch a glimpse of the overwhelming benefits of Sabbath-keeping, we would be falling over ourselves to take hold of it!

In the Daley household these days, our Sundays are defined by sleeping in a bit, sharing a big breakfast and a leisurely morning of sitting around the table drinking coffee and enjoying one another, attending the later worship service, spending the afternoon reading, playing quiet games with the kids, making phone calls to distant friends, perhaps taking a walk or a family bike ride, and then spending an evening by the fire or outside on the patio. For us, these expressions of worship, fellowship, and recreation are the essence of Sabbath.

A VERSUS B

Some of our attitudes and our approaches to work are shaped by our temperaments and personalities. Type A's are typically more self-starting, more motivated by accomplishment, and more inclined to busyness while Type B's are typically more laid back, more drawn to process than production, and more focused on relationships. Because of these characteristics, soulspace could be mistakenly viewed as nothing more than a template for Type B–ness (or a manifesto for my own personality orientation).

I think that perspective would be a mistake, and I'll tell you why. First and most importantly, the pillars of soulspace are not drawn from my experience and then propped up by Scripture; instead they are drawn from Scripture and reinforced by my own experience. Second, I intend no slight upon those who are Type A's. We don't get to choose our personalities; God does that, and what He chooses is good. Type A's and Type B's need each other, and each tends to eventually get miscalibrated without the other's vital perspectives. Third, every personality profile has its strengths and weaknesses, and the key to becoming an effective Kingdom-builder lies in utilizing our strengths and shoring up our weaknesses. So if you are an A, rejoice in the vital strengths you have while allowing the message of soulspace to wash over you—tempering your imbalances and envisioning your life as an A with space! If you are a B, rejoice in your natural tendency toward space, finding your balance by expressing your *being* in purposeful *doing*.

> *Type A's and Type B's need each other, and each tends to get miscalibrated without the other one's vital perspectives.*

Generally speaking, most facets of soulspace are going to come more easily to Type B's than A's. B's are going to "get it" first; they will more quickly see the value of soulspace and more readily adapt their lifestyles around this mind-set. A's may fight the notions of space, perhaps violently. But we all need space, A's and B's alike.

That said, I want to add that space may not look the same in the life of an A and a B, nor need it. While soulspace consists of a common set of values and practices, they will be lived out in ways that are as unique as are our personalities. My goal is not uniformity but awakened movement: the awakening of a vision and measurable movement toward that vision! We each have our own journey to make in the realm of the soul. Yet we can all benefit from one another and learn lessons that will aid us in our own journeys. So I hope that, whether you're an A or a B, you will be able to appreciate these perspectives on work, be challenged to evaluate your own soul honestly and openly, and be inspired toward Kingdom blessings in your work experience.

My goal is the awakening of a vision and measurable movement toward that vision.

WORK YOUR SPACE

We can apply the Kingdom pattern of working with space in three guiding principles: (1) actual priorities, (2) effective boundaries, and (3) contagious contentment.

Intended Versus Actual Priorities

The idea of priorities gets a lot of press, and rightly so. What is most important to us shapes the choices and decisions we make each day and, in so doing, shapes our very lives . . . and maybe even the lives of those around us. Great problems occur, however, when our *intended priorities* and our *actual priorities* are in conflict with one another. The greatest problem is deception: when we think we are living by a certain set of priorities but, in fact, live by another.

A lifestyle of space builds in to our days and years a quality of reflection and evaluation that makes it much easier to discover the disconnects between who we think we are and who we actually are. This is paramount to moving toward actual priorities, which reflect our true values. Consider mandating for yourself a structure of "workspace": inserting pockets of space into every week, month, quarter, and year where you honestly appraise your priorities against your actual history. Maybe you decide to take one hour per week, one day per month, a weekend per quarter, and a week each year, all for the purpose of evaluating where you have been, where you want to go, what priorities are true to your heart, and which ones have been assumed out of other people's expectations.

Should you attempt this kind of tangible application of workspace, prepare to be bombarded with every conceivable tactic—from others and from yourself—to derail the effort! And if you're not deeply convinced of the governing value of the exercise, it's better to not even try it. Remember, real change works from the inside out; external "time-management" principles will usually be subconsciously sabotaged by your deeper beliefs and habits.

Foundational to the concept of

External "time-management" principles will usually be subconsciously sabotaged by your deeper beliefs.

soulspace is the conviction that we *can* live the life we are meant to live. We *can* live on purpose. We need not live by the dictates of society and culture. Once again I must clarify that life neither can nor should be free from obstacle, pain, and difficulty. Those attributes are part of a world fallen from its heavenly design, and in the providence of God often become the vehicles themselves of growth and transformation. But if we can live not by accident but intentionally in the pursuit of God, our families, and our true selves—then we will actually live out our desired priorities.

Fighting the War to Set Boundaries

In reality, our world is full of *competing* priorities. Your priorities may compete with your co-worker's . . . or your boss's . . . or with those of the corporate culture you work within . . . or your in-laws'. . . or your industry's . . . or the media's . . . etc. In other words, there is constant, unrelenting pressure upon us all to yield our space to the priorities of other people and to be shaped, either in our personal lives or in our work worlds, into something different than our true hearts and callings. To call it a "war" is not to overdramatize the reality, and war calls for courage!

There is only one thing that can keep you true to your own inner compass in the face of these competing forces, and that is setting courageous boundaries: "Nnnnnnnnn . . . no!" Practice saying that ten times slowly as you drive to work each morning! The more skillful we can become at setting polite, respectful, but determined boundaries around our work worlds, the more effective we will become at advancing our unique assignments in the Kingdom of God on planet earth.

Of course, unless you own your own business, your personal boundaries have to operate within the requirements of your position. If you are hired as a receptionist, you can't set a boundary against accepting phone calls. But you can set a boundary against working overtime if that additional time will rob your family and intrude upon your priorities. Most workers face one of two challenges: the pull toward being rebellious—either inwardly or outwardly working in opposition to the expectations of their bosses—or the pull toward being a slave—indiscriminately acquiescing to all expectations of their bosses.

These are not always easy issues to resolve, balancing the need to operate within corporate boundaries and still honoring our own. We must honestly evaluate whether our personal priorities can function with integrity in our current work positions . . . and be willing to pursue other options if the answer is no. It's a rare blend of courage and faith that doesn't allow itself to be locked into what is safe and known. Without boundaries in our lives, space is merely an elusive wish.

The Power of Contentment

Contentment is one of the least regarded but most powerful keys to the Kingdom! Jesus taught this lesson in another Kingdom parable that again opens a window into the rules by which heaven operates and provides valuable insights, particularly for workspace. The story goes that the owner of a vineyard (it's an indication of how common wine was to the people of Jesus' time that He used it in so many stories) went out and successively hired workers throughout the day: at 6:00 A.M., 9:00 A.M., 12:00 P.M., 3:00 P.M., and finally at 5:00 P.M. (This sounds suspiciously like a word problem in junior high math, doesn't it?) At six o'clock that evening, the owner went out to pay his men. Starting with the first workers, he paid them a fair day's wage, but then he proceeded to pay each of the other workers the exact same amount! As you might imagine, the first workers were not happy, complaining loudly of injustice. But in truth, the owner's actions were entirely just toward the early workers; it was the later workers who received, not justice, but grace—much more than they deserved.

Without boundaries in our lives, space is merely an elusive wish.

The undercurrent in this story, told in Matthew 20:1–16 and reinforced by several other biblical passages (see 1 Timothy 6:6–11; Luke 3:14; Philippians 4:11–12; Hebrews 13:5–6), is that contentment empowers a man or woman to enjoy the goodness of God expressed in an honest wage for honest work. Contentment cuts across our natural inclinations toward complaint, animosity, and contention. As an added bonus, it releases a joy that is absolutely contagious. Contentment is attractive because it creates happiness. In contrast, discontent robs us of the joys of today in its ceaseless search for a better tomorrow. It undermines our core rest in the goodness and faithful provision of our heavenly Father.

To be fair, I have cultivated your discontent throughout this book. I have fed your frustration with the status quo, so now I need to make a clear delineation between a righteous and unrighteous discontent. The quality of the gift hinges upon the giver. What comes from God should be received with grateful contentment; in contrast, the things we have received by default from the world system should be met with divine discontent! Your schedule, your relationships, your financial status, even your job—these items have been defined by either a heavenly system or a worldly system. Determining the origin of the various parts will allow you to live a life of contentment as you seek to change elements of discontent. Even if you are in the absolute worst job, you can rest contentedly in fellowship with the awesome God of the universe while still harnessing a righteous discontent to push you toward your true Kingdom fit.

Incidentally, these three applications of workspace—actual priorities, courageous boundaries, and contagious contentment—all cut at the very roots of the world system. The honest appraisal of our true priorities cuts across our tendency toward pride and arrogance. Taking a courageous stance for Kingdom boundaries in our lives defeats the power of fear to control us. And contentment strikes a lethal blow to the underlying greed that seeks to drive our pace and dissipate our attention.

KINGDOM INVASION

It is my deep belief that you can shape your work with the quality of space. Work does not need to define your life with frantic busyness, anxiety, and chaos. With a commitment to space of soul, you can put 100 percent of your energy into your labors with the confidence that your work is set upon a foundation of unceasing faith, humility, and love. That is a recipe for a healthy soul—a soul empowered to face the inevitable difficulties and conflicts of work life with the power of the Holy Spirit.

Even if your job is less than ideal, you can turn that place into a Kingdom invasion through prayer and intercession, through the selfless serving of others, and through living the freedom of soul others

> *Actual priorities,*
> *courageous boundaries,*
> *and contagious*
> *contentment all cut at*
> *the very roots of the*
> *world system.*

desire to obtain. Until God opens the doors to a truer calling, activate your spiritual gifts to help change the climate of your workplace—*now!* People are hungry for space, and most will be drawn to its heavenly aroma in your life. As they observe you playing by different rules, they will either hate you or love you. Sorry, but it's the truth.

Finally, it's normal to feel something of a tug of war between work and home. It's akin to the periodic struggle between *being* and *doing.* But if we can keep the perspective that *being* is the defining force for meaningful *doing,* then I believe we will be empowered to protect the priority and health of the home as the potent base for meaningful work. Work—play—rest. We are designed for all three in balanced harmony. I can't say that my life is always described as "balanced harmony," but I can say in all truth that soulspace has dramatically increased both the balance and harmony of my life. And that's a good thing.

SOULSPACE PRESCRIPTION

Schedule a day now, as soon as three weeks out but no later than six, as a workspace day where you can spend that entire day evaluating the Kingdom components of your work situation (partnership, passion, space, and Sabbath). If your environment doesn't allow for this kind of flexibility, take a vacation day. I promise it will be worth your time. If you are in a leadership position, lead your department in a workspace event together.

chapter eleven

Save Me,
I'm a Pastor!

The noonday devil of the Christian life is the temptation to lose
the inner self while preserving the shell of edifying behavior.

—BRENNAN MANNING

MINISTRY IS SOME OF THE HARDEST and most rewarding
work in the world!

Many years ago, I was leading a worship team as a new pastor
and attending to the many details of organizing equipment, planning practices, learning songs, and—one of the biggest challenges—
finding decent musicians and singers (I was only semidecent
myself). One of my singers was a lady I really enjoyed having on our
worship team because she radiated the joy of the Lord and was very
demonstrative in her worship, something I think is crucial to leading
others in worship. However, her style of dress tended to be somewhat flamboyant, and one Sunday morning she wore a pair of tight
black pants that were shrink-wrapped to her lower body. I was
uncomfortable with her appearance, and after getting some well-
placed comments following the service, I figured it was my painful
duty as a leader to address the problem.

Okay, I nervously wondered, *how does one go about telling a lady that her pants are too tight, that instead of leading folks into worship, she might be leading them into other, less holy imaginations? Ah!* it came to me. *I don't tell her at all; I just tell her husband and let him deal with it.* Brilliant. Fabulous. Can't lose.

Well, I lost! She was terribly humiliated and didn't understand why I wouldn't talk to her personally about it instead of going "over her head." I stumbled over my apologies, trying to downplay the whole issue. She and her husband actually left the church over that one.

Are we having fun yet?

It was only a few months later when another crisis began to brew. This time it appeared that one woman in the church was criticizing the church leadership to another woman, and guess who was elected to make the pastoral visit?! *No problem,* I thought. *I learned my lesson last time: Don't go to the husband, go straight to the lady, right? Right.*

So I met the woman out in her front yard; her husband was at work. Are you cringing yet? Although I was sweating bullets, we had a fairly pleasant discussion in which I encouraged her to go directly to the leaders if she had difficulties to work through. Oh no, she assured me, it was all a simple misunderstanding.

The call I got that evening from her husband was anything but pleasant. He laid out in no uncertain terms that in the old days, when someone challenged the honor of his woman, the matter was settled by a duel! As my palms got sweaty and I stammered around like Elmer Fudd, I found myself grateful that sword-carrying was a century behind me. But trauma and wounding in ministry are anything but gone!

I know that many in pastoral min- istry endure much worse ordeals than occasional embarrassment or criticism. Many are horribly abused, often having their lives and the reputations of their families destroyed for generations to

As long as humans are involved, church will be a messy business.

come. Many pastors and spiritual leaders pour out their lives in daily fashion, running from one catastrophe to another, bearing the brunt of people's pain or anger with little thanks and less compensation. Of course, on the other hand, it is not uncommon for people in the church to be terribly hurt by those in spiritual leadership. The tragic bottom line is that the church can be the very antithesis of its calling to heal and restore.

GOD AND HIS MESSY CHURCH

As long as humans are involved, church will be a messy business. Nevertheless, God has chosen His church to be the primary vehicle for bringing His Kingdom to earth—not the church as a building or an organization, but the church as people. God's people. Our ability to love one another and care for each other will determine the pace at which God's Kingdom is planted in this earthly realm.

All the sons and daughters of God are ministers of God, endowed with spiritual gifts and a heart of compassion to live not for their own individual welfare but to live for the good of others, to live for the blessing and redemption of the community. It is my heart to apply the principles of space to the realm of Christian ministry, both to those in full-time church positions and to the rest of us who are called to serve in other ways. Whether you have been in professional

Christian ministry for twenty years or have simply considered leading a small group in your home, you will find valuable concepts in this chapter that will assist your calling.

Everything I communicated on the topic of work in the last chapter applies equally to full-time Christian work: the call to partnership, passion, space, and Sabbath, and the need for priorities, boundaries, and contentment. The rules don't change. But the challenge to heed them gets harder.

FULL-TIME SPACE

In rock climbing, a sport I picked up after moving to Colorado, every route has something called a *crux*. Quite simply, it's the hardest part of the route: maybe where the rock overhangs the climber like a small, or not so small, roof. Maybe it's the part where all the nice cracks and lips in the rock that you use for holds disappear and you're climbing on pure friction. But if you can get past the crux, then you have a clear route and can just enjoy the rest of the climb.

In my experience, the crux in ministry is coming to the heart revelation that God and ministry are not the same thing. Sounds simple enough, but it isn't always so. How do you say no to one more hurting person? How do you set any kind of meaningful boundaries on your time when we're talking about people's lives in the balance? And when is ministry ever finished? (For the answers to this quiz, turn your paper upside down and read the bottom line. Just kidding.)

In fact, the answers are easy to state, but they can be overwhelmingly difficult to apply: Honestly. Intentionally. Never.

On an emotional level, it usually feels like saying no to more ministry is saying no to God, and who can say no to God? On the other hand, when we can't say no we are easily sucked into shades of a savior complex only to feel that we have a responsibility and duty to save the world.

Recently a pastor shared an amazing story with me. Late one afternoon, a phone call was routed to his office from a distraught woman declaring that she was going to commit suicide that very hour. The pastor paused, took a breath, and said sincerely, "If you're going to kill yourself, why not do it the way Paul did it and give your life away to Christ? I agree, you need to die, but do it right. If you insist on being selfish and physically killing yourself, then at least do it with some consideration for your family. Try not to make a huge mess; that way, when your husband or children find you they'll be able to clean things up without too much trauma."

It usually feels like saying no to more ministry is saying no to God!

Stunned for a brief moment, the woman launched a shocked tirade at this unfeeling, insensitive pastor who she thought would at least be kind! But apparently it was the wrong time of the day for the "kindness" she wanted.

The pastor continued by telling the woman she was sadly self-absorbed and heartless to consider her life her own to waste—that Christ needed her life and she was incredibly selfish to inflict her death upon her family and friends. Back and forth the argument escalated until the woman lost all thought of killing herself because of her overwhelming rage at the pastor!

The next weekend she came to the Sunday service to personally confront the man with such despicable behavior . . . except she didn't get that far. When she met the pastor face to face her heart softened, and today, years later, she happily serves in the church, grateful for the safety she found because of the brutally honest confrontation with the pastor she now supports.

As I listened to this story, I just shook my head in awe—awe at God and His redeeming mercy, and awe at this pastor and his nerve! Now, neither he nor I would pretend that this would be the appropriate response to every distraught caller, but the point the story makes is astounding. First of all, we really must come to say with John the Baptist, "He must increase, but I must decrease" (John 3:30 KJV). In other words, there is a Savior, and I am not it! We can lead folks to the Living Water, but we can't make them drink. We can't drink for them. We can counsel them to drink; we can describe what will happen if they drink or if they don't. But people have to take responsibility for their own lives.

Healing Our Hyper-responsibility

Jesus exhibited this truth dramatically in His encounter with the "rich young man." In Mark 10:17–23, this man fell on his knees before Jesus in great sincerity, honoring Jesus as a "good teacher" and asking Him how to inherit eternal life.

Far from being callous to the man's need and desire, Mark's account says that Jesus "looked at him and loved him" (v. 21). But He challenged the man to give up his dependence upon money by giving away his wealth . . . and the young man wouldn't "drink"! Even though Jesus has the best claim of all to a Savior complex, He let the young man go. Imagine that! No running after him, no pleading. Instead of opening the door wide, Jesus narrowed it to a crack . . . to see what the man would do.

As spiritual leaders, we must put to rest our tendencies to become hyper-responsible for other people's welfare. We should serve, we should love, and we should care for people deeply and compassionately, but we must not cross the boundary line and tinker with their own domain of personal responsibility. This commitment in itself will be a great asset in guarding the space in our lives as ministers. It's a matter of not thinking of ourselves more highly than we ought, as Paul said in Romans 12:3. Or, in more contemporary language, don't take yourself too seriously!

As we relinquish the compulsion to live our lives based on other people's expectations of us and as we relinquish the compulsion to minister in order to satisfy our inner need to be needed, we begin to find space in ministry. And space is what we must have if we are to go the distance. You have to stop using the ax if you are to sharpen it, and a dull ax is no fun! To be effective in serving those God has placed in our keeping, we must set courageous boundaries to preserve our physical and emotional resources.

KEEPING FIRST THINGS FIRST

Deeper even than the need for pastors' personal renewal is the responsibility to protect our spouses from becoming ministry widows (and widowers) and our children from becoming emotionally orphaned! Our families will always be our first and most important ministry, and when that ceases to be true, we forfeit the right to lead others (see 1 Timothy 3:4–5). It is absurd to think we can coach others into having a healthy family life if ours is not. The reputation of PKs (pastors' kids) is that they are frequently the worst of the lot. I believe that is largely due to the neglect of fathers (or mothers) who are consumed with an unending string of meetings, appointments, preparations, obligations, and visitations.

Our families will always be our first and most important ministry.

For those in full-time ministry, evenings become a black hole of activity, sucking them into night after night of this and that: elders' meetings, small-group meetings, Wednesday night services, board meetings, missions meetings, finance meetings, recovery-group meetings, newcomers' meetings, discipleship meetings . . . Need I go on? And the weekends are no better; that's when normal people are off work, so that's when you visit and counsel and have more meetings! These are very important but demanding jobs.

Unfortunately, evenings and weekends are also the times when your children are out of school and need both Mom and Dad to do family stuff. These are the times when our spouses most need our assistance with the family. Yes, there is a special calling and grace upon families who are in ministry, but it is up to us to steward that grace well and assure above all else that our families are number one, not just in intention but in reality! Our priorities are demonstrated in what we do, not in what we say. We have no second chance to raise our kids; it has to be done right the first time.

The challenges to space of soul and family in a ministry home are enormous. It is time for a generation of spiritual leaders to ditch the pattern of failed marriages, lost kids, and ravaged souls and carve out a new model! That model is intimacy—deep, lasting, penetrating intimacy with God that yields the fruit of deep, lasting, penetrating intimacy in our marriages and families. There is no substitute. It's easier to preach to others how to do it than to do it. But do it we must if we are to be the Kingdom leaders for which we were created.

Prayer = Relationship

I have told you a number of things *not* to do in full-time ministry: Don't try to be people's savior. Don't work to prove yourself valuable. Don't neglect your family. Now here is something *to* do: Pray! I know, I know, you've read the books, and you've gone to the conferences. But do you pray? Or maybe a better question is, *How* do you pray? What is your motivation and objective?

Prayer's first priority is not about covering your list or covering your people. Prayer is first and totally foremost about spending time with your heavenly Lover—about lavishing your love on Him and drinking in His river of love for you! Prayer is all about relationship and not about production.

> *It's time for a generation of spiritual leaders to carve out a new model.*

It never ceases to amaze me how we can twist every God-given gift into just another attempt to produce something to justify our existence. We have nothing to justify, nothing to prove. Between our being formed to look like God and our being the object of heaven's greatest rescue, between being the house of the Holy Spirit and being chosen to marry God—our worth should be forever established.

If I were to tell you who are in full-time ministry that from this day forward, you had no choice but to spend one entire day each week in prayer—not writing a sermon, not counseling, not working on reading through the Bible in a year, not answering e-mail, but just spending time with your God—what feelings would arise? *That's unrealistic! Who are you kidding? Do you think I have a staff of ten? How would it all get done? What would I even do for an entire day alone with God?* Scary, isn't it? Let me say this: If you can't actually consider it, I suggest that admission is strong evidence that you are caught in a web of performance-oriented Christianity and are spreading that very virus to the people you lead.

Whether you choose to devote a day a week to prayer is not really my point, though I can think of nothing that would more deeply change the landscape of the American church. My point is that most of us need fairly radical movement to knock us out of our rut of pastor-by-the-numbers. I have found that my work takes on a life of its own, the life of the Spirit actually, when it is done within an ongoing atmosphere of prayer. For example, I blend my writing into my prayer days so that I am praying then writing, writing then praying—carrying on a more-or-less continuous conversation with God. Sometimes it is a holy flow, and sometimes it's hard work; but for sure it's a different way of living and ministering than anything I have touched before. So I commend this thinking to you, to prayerfully and boldly personalize this dynamic into your own ministry!

> *Most of us need fairly radical movement to knock us out of our rut of pastor-by-the-numbers.*

Equipping Others

Another key principle that pastors and leaders are beginning to rediscover is Jesus' brilliant plan of discipleship. It is not the pastor's job to tend the flock; it is the pastor's job to equip the flock to tend one another. If we get this—and if our people get this—then the pressure is off for us to be the resident professional "doer"! Our task then becomes training and equipping our people with the tools to lead their families, small groups, whatever.

And by the way, this practice is also preeminently biblical. Just look at Ephesians 4:11–12: "It was he who gave some to be apostles, some to be prophets, some to be evangelists, and some to be pastors and teachers, to prepare God's people for works of service, so that the body of Christ may be built up." In addition, it is preeminently healthy, because it opens the door to space. Soulspace.

Cultivate an Environment of Space

Lead your people into individual space by cultivating an environment of space through your leadership. Help them discover the joys of Sabbath-keeping by moving meetings and services away from Sunday afternoons and Sunday evenings. As ministry events and groups multiply in the church, relax the expectations that everyone who is spiritual needs to attend everything; let people be drawn into their passion instead of having to support yours. Don't take advantage of the dear hearts

> *Help your people simplify their lives instead of burdening them with more religious activities.*

who are serving- or mercy-motivated—the ones who will always say yes to every need for volunteers. Create an atmosphere of freedom in worship rather than a tightly controlled, choreographed performance. Encourage ideas and events that facilitate both solitude and community. Help your people simplify their lives instead of burdening them with more religious activities.

CREATING SPACE IN PART-TIME MINISTRY

It needs to be said that part-time ministry is not easy, either. By necessity part-time ministry usually occurs in the off-hours, those hours between work and bed, between weekend errands and home repairs—hours that are pulled in too many different directions already. Rather than tacking ministry tasks onto our already full to-do lists, we should go into part-time ministry by first considering who we are.

This self-knowledge begins by understanding our spiritual gifts. God is a giver, and it's His very nature to share Himself with us. He does this by apportioning specific facets of His own character and imparting them to us. Serving, teaching, encouraging, prophesying, giving—these are just a few of the godly deposits that emerge within our souls as gifts of the Spirit (see Romans 12:6–8 and 1 Corinthians 12:7–11). These gifts build upon, but are more than, our natural abilities. Isn't it amazing that God intends to manifest Himself to the world through these expressions of Himself in us!

Sometimes people have never considered their spiritual gifts because they have not been taught to do so. Sometimes they don't know their gifts because the windows of their souls are so constricted by clutter and soul sickness that the Spirit is barely flowing. Sometimes people are afraid to even believe that God could use them in creative ways. Whatever the reason, if we are to bring God's Kingdom to earth, we have to know our equipment. We need to understand how God wants to use us. If we don't, we may just be drawn into the most pressing need in our faith community. It's not that this is bad, per se, but if it's not a good fit, then the grace won't be there and it will diminish our soulspace. On the other hand, when we apply our God-given gifts in ministry, we find that our souls are actually refreshed and enlarged in the process. Amazing!

If you want assistance in determining your spiritual gifts, there are many books and questionnaires available that can help you hone in on your unique blend. As a starting point, you can check our web site at *www.soulspace.com* for a list of recommended resources.

By ministering through our spiritual gifts we learn to resist other pressures. When there's an urgent need in the church for help with a vital ministry, it's okay to jump in and help out temporarily, gifted or not. But set time limits: I'll help in the soup kitchen for a month. I'll pitch in with the nursery this weekend. But don't get permanently placed in positions for which you have no passion or calling. Furthermore, not all church ministries are essential; it's not necessarily helpful to artificially prop up a ministry of the church that has no sustainable base of support. Those who are "responders" by nature can easily wind up serving another person's passion and neglecting their own divine assignments. To correct this misdirection, the "market" should be allowed to weed out ministry ideas that aren't supportable at a given time while reinforcing ministries that God is blessing with widespread participation.

Which brings us right back to boundaries. My heart for your part-time ministry is this: Know what your calling is, pursue it, and don't be distracted by other needs and opportunities.

SOULSPACE PRESCRIPTION

Carve out a thirty-minute block sometime today or tomorrow and get totally alone. Spend ten minutes with your eyes closed, not praying but just letting your heart be filled with the presence of Jesus. Then, during the next ten minutes, ask the Lord what He has made you to be in His house—what your gifts and callings are—and if you are using them. Spend the final ten minutes writing down ideas for extricating yourself from giftless ministry and initiating gifted ministry.

chapter twelve

An Invitation to Journey

All I want is Your grip on my heart.
All I need is Your face in mine.
All I want to do is feast my soul on You
Every day of my life.

—J. D.

YOU MAY NOT HAVE REALIZED when you first picked up this book that you were picking up a ticket to undiscovered territory. Perhaps you are an experienced traveler into the unknown, or perhaps you're someone who has just recently realized that there is indeed a big world lying just outside the city limits of your history. Somewhere along the path that wound through these pages, I hope you realized that God has much to say and much to show and that He is, in fact, constantly speaking to us and revealing things to us . . . if we will but pay attention.

This book is about paying attention.

My wife and I got a good lesson in "attention" in November 2000 as we attended a class taught by author Ken Gire. He gathered our group together one morning to retrace our steps toward the lobby of the building we had entered moments before. He halted us suddenly before a painting of a lion, one we had passed dozens of times without stopping.

"Look at it," he said. And look we did. Five minutes went by. Ten minutes. We all stood there, captivated by the intricate web of lines that wove together the face of majestic grandeur, beautifully capturing something of the sorrow and nobility of this king of beasts.

Attention. Is it a quality you have cultivated? How many times has God called to you from beside the beaten track of your daily obligations only to have you fly by without a glance? How often has God been poised to break into our worlds but there was no space?

It is my hope that during our time together, I have blown upon the glowing embers of a vision within you, a vision to live by another set of rules than those you see mirrored around you every day. I hope you've seen how you can begin to capture a hope and make it real in your day-in, day-out world, even as Kellie and I seek it in ours. My goal has been to lay out for you the reasons, both theological and practical, that space is the path to truly living in the purpose of God and living true to your own design. My desire has been to awaken within you the hope for change and determination to shake off the imprint of a soul-sick world, to forge a path both ancient in vision yet modern in application.

Throughout these pages I have tried to share our story—a story of redemption from the insidious grasp of clutter and busyness toward a life of freedom and purpose. Don't for a second think that Kellie and I now have it all figured out or that our life together now has that surreal, sepia-tinged, Mayberry-like equilibrium to it. As many have said before, life is a journey. Some days are ripe with destiny; others are rife with difficulty. But I no longer feel like life has got me by the tail and won't let go—at least, not often. More frequently I feel like God has me by the heart, and I'm trying to relax in His safe grip!

Each day you and I will build our lives with one of two

systems—on the sand or on the Rock, out of straw or out of bricks, by the rules of the world system or by those of heaven. My deep conviction is that soulspace is an important missing ingredient in today's world, and it's missing as much from the church as from anywhere. Space isn't everything. But it's hard to do anything well without it.

I hope I have put words to feelings you have had but could not define. I hope I have encouraged, perhaps inspired, maybe riled, but at least connected with you on matters of the heart in a way that empowers you onward toward the quest and toward God Himself.

In the movie *Braveheart,* William Wallace makes many profound statements, but none better than this: "Every man dies; not every man really lives!" It's in my heart, and I believe in yours, that we would be counted among the few who really live. There is no comprehensive how-to on this journey. We have to walk the road ourselves and learn as we go. But thankfully, we don't walk alone; we have companions on the journey. We share the grace of learning from one another along the way, giving and receiving hard-won wisdom. And we go with God.

PRESUMPTIONS AND PURPOSES

I have presumed several things of you in your soul search. First, I believe there is something within you that says, *I was made for significance. My life is supposed to count for something big.* Second, I expect you know your significance is somehow bound up with who God is and the Story He has written. Third, I suspect you are frustrated—mildly or severely—with the clutter of life that keeps you trapped in insignificance.

Believe it or not, frustration can be a good thing. Even anger can be good in that it yells at us and says, *Wake up! Something is wrong here. This isn't the way it's supposed to be!* Anger, like guilt, is a guardian of our souls to awaken us to action. If we don't respond to anger and guilt with appropriate action, these emotions turn rancid and pollute our lives with bitterness and shame. But properly used, they rouse us from apathy and motivate us toward solutions.

John Eldredge rightly stated, "Christianity has nothing to say to the person who is completely happy with the way things are. . . . You cannot help someone who does not want a thing."[1] Dissatisfaction, then, either causes us to lower our expectations to something more manageable, something more available to us right now, or it motivates us to reach.

This book is about reaching.

But what, you may rightly wonder, *am I reaching for? What is the destination of this journey?*

Our journeys themselves lead to the End of all things, who is also the Beginning—the King of kings, the Lord of lords, the Giver of life, the Lover of our souls. Our journeys lead to God Himself. This book, on the other hand, has more modest purposes: (1) that we will become able to see and be motivated to look for the things that clutter and poison our souls, (2) that we will realize that we do have choices and the power to make the choice for space, and (3) that the lasting rewards to be found in soulspace will become far more compelling than our brief flings with clutter and distraction.

What is it exactly that we want to make space for in our lives?

My goal is to help you make room for what is truly most important in your life, as I'm striving to do in mine.

Let me take a moment to tell you what soulspace is not. Soulspace is not simply a good feeling about life, although it will improve your quality of life. Soulspace is not about disconnecting from real life, although in creating space in your soul you may be led to disconnect from life as you know it. Soulspace is not ethereal and intangible, yet it resists simplistic definitions. Soulspace is not so much a destination as it is the power to shape your journey.

If you are looking for a quick fix—six days to inner peace, no drastic changes required—then you will be disappointed. Soulspace is not about time management but about priority management. It's not about getting more done but about working on the right things to begin with. It's not about efficiency but effectiveness. In a few years, what will still matter—that extra meeting and phone call you crammed in today, or hunting June bugs with your daughter? The day may not allow both, so you have to make choices, for better or worse, for richer or poorer.

This book is about choosing to be rich.

A HOPE AND A CALLING

Great things await those who will press past all obstacles and take hold of who they really are and what God has really called them to in life. But there is a price to pay for both the pursuit of and the obtaining of soulspace. It is a wonderful and dangerous journey. There are things now hidden in your soul, things that you are probably not anxious to deal with, that will come to light once the clutter that so effectively hides them is gone. There are fears and insecurities that will get stirred up. Suppressed dreams, desires, and longings will clamor to be addressed in meaningful ways. Past injuries and hurts may require going back into an unresolved past. Your own failures and disappointments may loom large.

But then again, what is the price of clutter? Too high, is my answer!

Everything that's worth anything costs something, so let's go! Let's do something. We can't do everything, but we can do something. Not everything in this book has your name on it, but something does—and you can do that something. One right choice made, one righteous step taken in the direction of space, and this book will have been worth the reading. Do not put it off. Do not be overwhelmed and paralyzed. Please start with something and live the life you were fashioned for! God is the strength of our lives and the power to change. If we ask, He will answer. If we seek, He will be found. Make a choice and take a step.

As I complete this writing, our road takes us full circle from Colorado back to North Carolina, where we will attempt to live out the life-giving truths we have discovered here in the land of mountains and sunshine. But we do not return the same. We feel as if we are very different people, truly changed from the inside out, with new perspectives, new priorities, and a refined vision. God has broken in.

Through this adventure, we have obtained enough space to discover more of who we are and why we are here. Armed with that vision, we have established an outreach called oneFlesh Ministries for the purpose of communicating God's deposit in us to others through writing, teaching, and worship, and through our websites—*www.soulspace.com* and *www.onefleshministries.org*—where additional resources are available. The name, oneFlesh Ministries, is more descriptive of who we are than what we do, and I like it that way!

As for what the road ahead holds for us, we don't know. But we feel more equipped for the journey than ever before and are excited about where the quest will take us. I am grateful for the chance to share this journey. You have heard some of our story; someday perhaps I'll get to hear part of yours. In the meantime, I offer a prayer for us all:

Father God, it is You who have fashioned us and set within us a hope and a calling . . . to know You, to know others, to know ourselves. We hear You beckon to us to leave behind the broken pieces we once held so dearly and to chart a new course, to take the risk of reaching for a life of significance through space of soul. Utterly dependent upon You, we seek to be men and women of the Kingdom, warriors and lovers for the sake of our Lord Jesus Christ. Amen.

acknowledgments

W HILE THE IDEAS IN THIS BOOK are interconnected with
the lives and messages of a host of people in my world, I
want to express unique gratitude to three people for their role in the
formation of *soul space*. First, my friend and agent Kathy Helmers
affirmed and focused my vision for this project, offering her energy
and experience to make the dream an amazing reality. Thank you so
much, Kathy, for your faith in this new writer.

In addition, two friends poured an unusual amount of themselves into our message and our personal journey of soulspace: Susy
Holloway and David Lobach. Your contributions to both life and
manuscript have enriched us in many ways, and Kellie and I are
deeply grateful.

Chapter 2. Stripped to the Bone, Regrounded in God

1. Jack Deere, *Theology of Intimacy with God,* Wagner Leadership Institute tape series, 9–11 November, 1999.

Chapter 3. The Clutter Strikes Back

1. Brent Curtis and John Eldredge, *The Sacred Romance* (Nashville: Thomas Nelson, 1997), 1.

2. Richard A. Swenson, M.D., *Margin* (Colorado Springs, Colo.: NavPress, 1992), 17.

3. Tommy Tenney, *The God Chasers* (Shippensburg, Pa.: Destiny Image Publishers, 1998), 26–27.

4. Swenson, *Margin,* 13.

5. Winston Churchill, from a speech given at the Lord Mayor's Luncheon, Mansion House, London, 10 November 1942.

Chapter 4. Breaking into the Closet

1. C. S. Lewis, *The Weight of Glory and Other Addresses* (Grand Rapids, Mich.: Eerdmans, 1965), 1–2, quoted in John Piper, *Desiring God: Meditations of a Christian Hedonist* (Portland, Oreg: Multnomah, 1986), 15–16.

Chapter 5. "With a Big Sky Over Me"

1. Scott Vaughn, "Somewhere in Montana" (Colorado Springs: Flying W Wranglers). Used by permission.

2. C. S. Lewis, *The Last Battle* (New York: MacMillan, 1956), 25.

3. Gil Bailie, quoted by John Eldredge, *Wild at Heart* (Nashville: Thomas Nelson, 2001), 200.

4. Gordon Dalbey, *Healing the Masculine Soul* (Dallas: Word, 1988), 28.

Chapter 6. Fix Me, I'm Broken

1. This idea comes from Ed Smith's theophostic video series and workbooks, *Beyond Tolerable Recovery* (Campbellsville, Ky.: Alethia Publishing, 1999).

2. C. S. Lewis, *The Voyage of the Dawn Treader* (New York: HarperCollins, 1952), 115–16.

Chapter 7. Cleaning House
1. Brennan Manning, *Ruthless Trust* (New York: Harper-San Francisco, 2000), 31–32.

Chapter 8. Into the Scary World of Intimacy
1. Manning, *Ruthless Trust,* 101–102.

2. Dan Allendar, *The Healing Path* (Colorado Springs: Waterbrook, 1999), 237, 246.

3. Ibid., 248.

4. Ibid., 249, 253.

5. Manning, *Ruthless Trust,* 100.

6. Jack Deere, lecture, "Theology of Intimacy with God, II," Wagner Leadership Institute, 9-10 November 2000.

Chapter 9. A Recipe for Energy—and Rest
1. Kenneth Barker, ed., *The NIV Study Bible* (Grand Rapids: Zondervan, 1995), 773.

2. *New Exhaustive Strong's Numbers and Concordance* (Biblesoft electronic version, 1994).

3. C. H. Spurgeon, *The Treasury of David,* vol. 1 (McLean, Va: MacDonald Publishing, n.d.), 27.

4. Ibid.

Chapter 10. Reworking Your Workspace
1. Dorothy C. Bass, "Rediscovering the Sabbath," *Christianity Today,* 1 September 1997, 40.

2. Ibid., 41, 43.

Chapter 12. An Invitation to Journey
1. John Eldredge, *The Journey of Desire* (Nashville: Thomas Nelson, 2000), 43, 56.